WALK-INS FROM A WORLD TO COME

Moses, Christ, Lincoln, and Gandhi were Walk-ins—enlightened beings who, after successfully completing numerous incarnations, attained sufficient awareness of the meaning of life to forego the time-consuming process of birth and childhood, returning directly to adult bodies.

IN *STRANGERS AMONG US,* YOU WILL:

- Meet actual Walk-ins, here to guide us into a fantastic new age...
- Discover that the energy locked in a grain of sand can power a major city for a year...
- Learn how to conjure up empty parking spaces on crowded streets, dissolve clouds, heal your friends, enjoy bountiful good health...
- Know how to prepare for the coming apocalypse when the axis of the Earth undergoes a radical shift...

STRANGERS AMONG US
AN INVALUABLE GUIDE
FOR THE AMAZING ERA AHEAD

Fawcett Crest Books
by Ruth Montgomery:

BORN TO HEAL

HERE AND HEREAFTER

STRANGERS AMONG US

THE WORLD BEFORE

A WORLD BEYOND

Ruth Montgomery

STRANGERS AMONG US

Enlightened Beings from
A World to Come

FAWCETT CREST • NEW YORK

To my friend

HOPE RIDINGS MILLER

A Fawcett Crest Book

Published by Ballantine Books

Copyright © 1979 by Ruth Montgomery

ISBN 0-449-20061-2

This edition published by arrangement with Coward, McCann & Geoghegan

Manufactured in the United States of America

First Fawcett Crest Edition: March 1982
First Ballantine Books Edition: June 1982

Contents

Foreword

Benjamin Franklin was a Walk-in, and like all such advanced souls he brought in with him Awareness. Because of this special quality, he perfectly understood the illusion of what we term "living," and the reality of the greater life that we call "death." His Awareness is exemplified in the letter that he wrote to Miss Hubbard on the occasion of the death of his brother, John Franklin:

PHILADELPHIA, 23d February, 1756.
I CONDOLE with you. We have lost a most dear and valuable relation. But it is the will of God and nature that these mortal bodies be laid aside when the soul is to enter into real life. This is rather an embryo state, a preparation for living. A man is not completely born until he be dead. Why, then, should we grieve that a new child is born among

the immortals, a new member added to their happy society?

We are spirits. That bodies should be lent us while they can afford us pleasure, assist us in acquiring knowledge, or in doing good to our fellow-creatures, is a kind and benevolent act of God. When they become unfit for these purposes and afford us pain instead of pleasure, instead of an aid become an incumbrance, and answer none of the intentions for which they were given, it is equally kind and benevolent that a way is provided by which we may get rid of them. Death is that way. We ourselves, in some cases, prudently choose a partial death. A mangled, painful limb which cannot be restored we willingly cut off. He who plucks out a tooth parts with it freely, since the pain goes with it; and he who quits the whole body parts at once with all pains and possibilities of pains and diseases which it was liable to or capable of making him suffer.

Our friend and we were invited abroad on a party of pleasure which is to last forever. His chair was ready first and he is gone before us. We could not all conveniently start together, and why should you and I be grieved at this, since we are soon to follow and know where to find him? Adieu,

B. FRANKLIN

Dr. Franklin, a scientist of international renown, also believed in Reincarnation, of which he wrote: "When I see nothing annihilated (in the works of God) and not a drop of water wasted, I cannot suspect the annihilation of souls, or believe that He will suffer the daily waste of millions of minds ready made that now exist, and put Himself to the continual trouble of making new ones. Thus, finding myself to exist in the world, I believe I shall, in some shape or other, always exist; and, with all the inconveniences human life is liable to, I shall not object to a new edition of mine, hoping, however, that the errata of the last may be corrected."

At the age of twenty-two, having already become a Walk-in, he wrote his own epitaph, which Carl Van Doren has called "the most famous of American epitaphs."

> The Body of B. Franklin,
> Printer,
> Like the Cover of an Old Book,
> Its Contents Torn Out
> And
> Stripped of its Lettering and Gilding,
> Lies Here
> Food for Worms,
> But the Work shall not be Lost,
> For it Will as He Believed
> Appear Once More
> In a New and more Elegant Edition
> Revised and Corrected
> By the Author.

And at the seasoned age of seventy-four, taking a long look into the as-yet-unturned pages of history, Ben Franklin wrote to Joseph Priestley, the discoverer of oxygen, as follows:

"It is impossible to imagine the height to which may be carried, in a thousand years, the power of man over matter. We may perhaps learn to deprive large masses of their gravity, and give them absolute levity, for the sake of easy transport. Agriculture may diminish its labour and double its produce; all diseases may by sure means be prevented or cured, not excepting even that of old age, and our lives lengthened at pleasure even beyond the antediluvian standard. O that moral science were in as fair a way of improvement, that men would cease to be wolves to one another, and that human beings would at length learn what they now improperly call humanity."

This book, through the aid of the Guides, will also take a long look forward to life one thousand years hence.

CHAPTER I

The Mystery of Walk-Ins

There are Walk-ins on this planet.

Tens of thousands of them.

Enlightened beings, who, after successfully completing numerous incarnations, have attained sufficient awareness of the meaning of life that they can forego the time-consuming process of birth and childhood, returning directly to adult bodies.

A Walk-in is a high-minded entity who is permitted to take over the body of another human being who wishes to depart. Since a Walk-in must never enter a body without the permission of its owner this is not to be confused with those well-publicized cases (such as were described in *The Three Faces of Eve, The Exorcist,* et al) in which

multiple egos or evil spirits are vying for possession of an inhabited body.

The motivation for a Walk-in is humanitarian.
He returns to physical being in order to help others
help themselves, planting seed-concepts that will
grow and flourish for the benefit of mankind.

Some of the world's greatest spiritual and political leaders, scientists, and philosophers in ages
past are said to have been Walk-ins, but during
these final decades of the twentieth century the
pace has been steadily accelerating, and many
more of them are entering mature physical bodies
to prepare us for the shift of the earth on its axis
at the end of the century, and the New Age that
is dawning.

Not all Walk-ins are towering leaders. Many
are working quietly among us today, going about
their unsung task of helping us to understand ourselves, to seek inner guidance, and to develop a
philosophy that will sustain us through the trying
times ahead.

You may know a Walk-in in your own office. Or
in your community. They seldom reveal themselves, because to do so would imperil the good
work for which they returned to physical being.

In fact, you yourself may be a Walk-in! Since
the memory pattern of the departing entity survives intact, Walk-ins are sometimes unaware of
their altered status for several years after the substitution has been effected.

Why have you never heard of Walk-ins before?

That is exactly what I asked myself when, while
recently reading a stack of fan mail, I found my

attention riveted by one paragraph in a beauti-
fully written letter. My unknown correspondent,
after mentioning that she was disappointed in
having found no new book by me for the past two
years, wrote:

"Are you looking for ideas for future books? I
would like to see what your unseen friends [mean-
ing my Guides] have to say about the role of Walk-
ins on the planet. As they will tell you, a Walk-in
is a highly evolved entity who, always with permission, enters the body of a human who wishes
to check out before completing the tasks he has
begun. Sometimes the human has lost heart, or
had taken on a task more difficult than he was
prepared to handle. Sometimes it was the purpose
of the departing human to begin the task and prepare the body for the new entity. The Walk-in first
completes the tasks of the body's previous owner,
and then goes on to do what he must do on his
own projects, which are really those of a gardener
who plants seeds on the planet, helps those seeds
to germinate, and then lets them grow in their
own direction. If you ask, your unseen friends will
tell you more. They will also mention political,
military, spiritual, and philosophical leaders who
were Walk-ins, who inspired or led people, and
who are remembered for what they started. Perhaps it is time to tell the story of these remarkable
beings, who are human while they are among us,
and who help us along the way in our own evolution."

Wow! The very idea was enough to blow the
mind!

In my long and laborious journey from a skeptical syndicated columnist on politics and world affairs, to a writer on subjects beyond the range of our five senses, I had finally become convinced of reincarnation. I had also come to accept that spirits, under certain circumstances, can briefly materialize before loved ones, and then eerily dissolve. I myself have never seen a spirit or heard other-world voices, but there no longer seems any reason to doubt the veracity of those highly credible persons who insist they have.

But Walk-ins? Human beings of flesh and blood who walk among us, confidently occupying a body that previously belonged to another? It seemed rather much to swallow. Yet the thought continued to tantalize my waking hours, and even to color my dreams. The correspondent, obviously well educated and intelligent, had indeed planted a seed; and after several days of restless wondering, I finally decided to seek counsel from my Guides, those unseen spirit friends who have been dictating through my typewriter from time to time since 1960.

Readers of my previous books in the psychic field are familiar with Lily, the mysterious spirit who directs my automatic writing, and with Arthur Ford, the famous American medium who joined Lily in my charmed circle of spiritual advisers after his death in 1971. They know that each morning after meditation, if I lightly rest my fingertips on the typewriter keys while still in the alpha state, the Guides write their messages and profound thoughts through me. Afterward, on reading what they have written, I am invariably impressed by their far-ranging knowledge and by the accuracy of their verifiable statements, but I must confess that of late I had grievously neglected them.

For one reason, my fingers were blistered from an unknown allergy that rendered them too sore for typing. For another, the Guides had been persistently urging that I write a book to help prepare readers for the coming shift of the earth on its axis, which they say will occur near the close of this century, after a devastating war. The thought, to me, is a chilling one, and since the Guides had touched on the subject in the closing chapters of *The World Before,* I felt deep reluctance to pursue it. (Could my unwillingness to cooperate have precipitated the allergy?) At any rate, the more the Guides persisted, the less tractable I became, until I eventually ceased the morning sessions altogether.

Then came the challenging letter from my unknown reader, whom I shall call Laura, and after mulling it over for a few days, I returned to the typewriter to consult the Guides. Are there, I asked, such things as Walk-ins on this planet, and was there any truth to the letter that I had received?

After my usual period of meditation, with eyes still closed, I touched the keys lightly, and the Guides began to write: "The so-called Walk-ins are superior souls who have gone on after many earthly lives, and some of them need not return but are doing so in order to help others. They wish to avoid returning as babies, and enduring the childhood state in which valuable time would be wasted, so they do indeed take over, with permission, the bodies of discouraged or willing souls who are ready to depart. Some are able to go directly to the purpose of their earthly return, and have become philosophers and research scientists, while some are as yet unaware that they were not always in the bodies they now inhabit. They make up a small but brilliant portion of today's society, and they will come in increasing numbers as the earth approaches the shift of the axis during the last part of this century.

"In past centuries Walk-ins have flowered and waned and come again, and they are a prime example of the immortality of the soul. Thus, those who attain to a sufficiently advanced level need not repeat the learning processes of birth, babyhood, and schooling in order to serve others. By electing to enter directly into an adult body no longer wanted by the occupant, they bring with them a deepened awareness, a fresher recollection of akashic records and goals to be reached, and are able to communicate personally with other earthlings, unlike the spirit entities who are ever-present but seldom seen or heard by those in physical body."

Here, then, seemed verification of the letter that had arrived at such a propitious time, when I was devoid of fresh ideas, and seemingly on a dry plateau. But why had the Guides never mentioned Walk-ins to me before?

"Because we had no intention," they wrote, "of

telling you about this subject until you were ready
to receive the information and develop curiosity
about it. It is an idea whose time has come."

After the morning session, I was just beginning
to read those words when the telephone rang. My
editor, Patricia Soliman, was on the line, asking
rather plaintively when I would be ready to get
back into harness and write another book. Patricia
and I always seem to be operating on the same
wavelength, and after I excitedly read to her the
paragraph from the letter that lay open on my
desk, she exclaimed, "Ruth, you should see my
goose bumps! I feel sure that the writer of that
letter is a Walk-in, although in all the manuscripts I've read in the psychic field I've never
heard of them."

The thought that a mysterious Walk-in might
actually be in touch with me had not occurred
until then, but after the Guides confirmed Patricia's hunch at the next day's session, I eagerly
responded to the woman's letter, making no mention of what my editor and the Guides had said
about her, but asking if I might come to see her.
After a short delay she graciously gave consent,
and two days later I flew to an area several
hundred miles from my home, taking the Guides'
written messages about Walk-ins with me.

The Guides had declared that Laura is a highly
evolved individual who became a Walk-in a year
ago, after the original occupant of the body, faced
with a seemingly insurmountable marital problem, elected to withdraw. Laura seemed stunned
as she read these words, and refused to confirm

that she was a Walk-in; but after we had spent several fascinating hours together, her barrier of reticence slowly began to crumble. She said she had certainly not thought of herself as a Walk-in when she contacted me, but had felt a strong inner compulsion to write as she did, "dangling a carrot" to encourage me to investigate a subject that she had heard about.

"I trusted you, and felt strongly that some of your own Guides were among a group around my typewriter as I wrote to you," she confessed, whereupon I showed her another message from the Guides that said: "We have worked with her [Laura] both on this side, and since she became a Walk-in last year."

Laura then said she had been made aware that two of her acquaintances were occupying bodies into which they had not originally been born, but she refused even to consider that she herself might be a Walk-in until the evening before my arrival, when two discarnates gave her the identical information that I had just brought her from my Guides. She permitted me to read excerpts from her private journal, which described the alteration in her personality and attitudes at the time of her divorce a year previously, and recorded that the evening before my visit, "I was told by discarnates that I had taken this body about a year ago. They who told me said that I needed this piece of information before meeting with Ruth, in order to field her questions with wisdom, for the greatest good of all."

The new Laura recounted fascinating details of

the gradual withdrawal of the old Laura, when for a time they seemingly took turns occupying the body, although never at the same time, until the substitution was completed to the satisfaction of both. But because she could vividly recall details from the old Laura's childhood and college years, she would not accept that the new Laura was a Walk-in, even after another Walk-in, who recognized her changed status, explained that there is no break in the memory pattern of the withdrawing entity when the replacement takes over.

Since that day when I had the first of many conversations with Laura, I have been privileged to speak with other Walk-ins, explicitly identified as such by the Guides and by their own inner knowing, and have learned that no such persons should be publicly identified while still in flesh, because to do so could hamper the purpose of their return to earthly being. They do not need ego trips! They come, not as masters or authorities, but as servants and workers whose task it is to help others discover Truth for themselves.

It seems that certain Walk-ins of the past can be revealed, but only if they are not presently reincarnated, since even that disclosure could affect their anonymity. To illustrate, the Guides told me that a genius of the nineteenth century, whose name is a household word, was a Walk-in, and that his inventions which have revolutionized our way of life were "transferred almost directly from the spirit plane to Planet Earth through the gigantic ability of this man." Yet I am not permitted to reveal his well-known name, because although he died some years ago he is said to have returned to flesh, and is presently engaged in work that should lead to another tremendous breakthrough, this time in the field of medicine.

By contrast, the Guides readily agreed to name some other Walk-ins, because they are not presently incarnate. Among them are:

● Mohandas K. Gandhi (1869–1948), "who rallied a slumbering giant [India] to action without benefit of sword," thereby freeing that nation.

● Benjamin Franklin (1706–1790), the printer, author, publisher, inventor, scientist, public servant, and diplomat, who has been called the first civilized American, and America's first world statesman.

● Abraham Lincoln (1809–1865), taking over from a country lawyer, "who after several traumatic experiences and violent headaches withdrew in favor of the lofty entity who entered that body, signed the Emancipation Proclamation, and sadly led America in a divisive but necessary war to free the countless souls trapped in slavery."

● Harvey Firestone (1868–1938), who virtually put the modern world on wheels by pioneering the manufacture of pneumatic and balloon tires.

● Emanuel Swedenborg (1688–1772), who, after having attained the highest pinnacle of scientific fame, "and propounding all that the world was prepared to understand or conceive at that time," willingly gave up earthly fame and fortune to step aside, so that a transcendental soul might use that well-known body to teach the oneness of the spiritual and physical world. The Guides say the new entity arrived after the experience in which the original entity (the scientist) saw the heavens opened wide, and realized that his own work was satisfactorily completed and that another would further the cause of mankind by taking over his physical body. "A prime example of the good that comes from Walk-ins arriving fully armed for their work as adults," the Guides added.

● Meister Eckhart (1260?–?1327), the German monk and scholastic mystic who taught that the goal of the human soul is union with God.

● Shankara (788?–?820), the dropout from Hinduism and leading exponent of Advaita Vedanta.

● Joseph, the Biblical Canaan lad with the coat of many colors, who, after being sold into slavery by jealous brothers, stepped aside for a highly evolved entity who interpreted the dreams of the Pharaoh, and rose to become a wise governor of Egypt.

● The Christ Spirit, who according to the Guides, became the greatest of the Walk-ins "at the time of the Nazarene's baptism, when God became manifest in the man Jesus." The Guides will have more to say about this later, but it is interesting to note that Edgar Cayce, the seer of Virginia Beach, also said that the Christ Spirit did not enter until Jesus was baptized by John the Baptist.

My spirit friends say that since a Walk-in automatically inherits the memories of the departing entity, he may continue for some time to identify himself with the John or Mary Doe he has replaced, but he will immediately begin to discover within himself a new awareness of life energies, deeper perceptions, clearer goals, and a love for all beings. The often muddled individual who vacated the body is replaced by one who intuitively knows how to solve the problems that blocked the other's progress. The Walk-in for a time may believe that he has simply been granted new insight, and because he has agreed before entering the body to complete the tasks begun by the Walk-out, few of his associates will suspect the substitution of egos.

Yet as time passes, and the person becomes more energetic, hopeful, and dedicated, relatives and friends will remark on the great improvement in his attitude. Passivity is gone, and with it the previous reluctance to attack new problems and find a way out of the despair or boredom. When such improvement occurs associates at first will marvel at the alteration but then will come to accept that the person has successfully passed through a period of depression.

Gradually, as old projects are completed, the Walk-in will move into new pathways, and when he realizes that he was not originally born into the body he now occupies, he will be irresistibly drawn to other Walk-ins who are already at work raising the level of humanity. In fact, they will seek him out, and help him in his adjustment.

And what of those who choose to vacate their bodies in favor of a Walk-in?

The Guides stress that a Walk-out is not a cop-out. No karmic penalty attaches to such a decision, for unlike a suicide, he is not destroying life.

In *A World Beyond* the Guides explained how

a soul, before reincarnating, elects to be born into a situation where he has the best opportunity to pay off old karmic debts and learn needed lessons. They have now lifted another curtain on the mystery of reincarnation by reporting that a soul who has wearied of the debilitating ailments of old age, after several lengthy lives, will sometimes volunteer to repeat the life cycles of babyhood and childhood, learning new lessons specifically to prepare the body for a more advanced entity who can enter it as a Walk-in. Sometimes, they say, a Walk-in will exchange places with an injured soldier on the battlefield or with a prisoner on death row in order to erase an entangling karma from a previous lifetime when he himself caused another's violent death or injury.

Ordinarily, however, the cases are less dramatic. Perhaps a person is discouraged by his seeming inability to resolve a distressing personal relationship, or he may be desperately ill. He may have lost a loved one through death, separation, or divorce, and have thereby lost his will to live. The Guides say of this situation: "Walk-ins are careful not to enter bodies where strong emotional ties to others are still present. In this way they avoid too-close alliances that may get in the way of the pursuit of their higher goals. In fact, those with strong ties to another living person are seldom ready to walk out of their bodies and let another step in. Those who are free from such intimate ties are more willing to make way for another to complete the life cycle of his physical body."

Whatever the reason, a Walk-out has always reached a point of transition before abandoning his body. And whether the person is a battered wife, a husband driven to distraction by a carping wife, a cripple, or one who has simply lost the will to live, a Walk-in cannot replace him unless he is willing to take over his unfinished tasks and master the problems, before launching his own projects.

Fully aware of the danger of a disturbed person's mind being taken over by one or more evil entities, I asked the Guides how one who was willing to relinquish his body could protect himself from that terror.

"By remaining God-centered, loving the Creator in oneself and others," they replied. "To protect oneself from evil spirits, mentally place a circle around oneself, filling it with golden light and breathing into it love and peace. The subconscious is a powerful instrument for helping us picture situations which we wish to develop. This aura of golden light enveloping one in the perfect circle of eternity is important in many ways, warding off evil and filling ourselves with tranquility. It erases fear, and protects us, and is a good course to follow each day at the beginning of meditation.

"When one decides to make his body available for a more highly evolved entity, he should picture himself floating off into space, while another sets up housekeeping in his vacated body. This will alert those on this side who wish to become Walkins, and will further expand one's own awareness. It is unnecessary to do this more than a few times before a high-minded entity will begin to make its presence felt. Warmth and love will radiate from it. But the vacater should not practice this unless he has definitely decided that he would like to return to spirit, and is willing to have his present incarnation carried on by another. The process is not a lengthy one. Depending on the condition of one's body and the readiness to depart, a few months at most are required by the Walk-in to study the akashic records of the departing soul, determine how to master the body, and understand the best ways for solving the dilemma in which the Walk-out has found himself."

Rereading this message at a later time, I was not sure that the directions were clear, so I asked the Guides if they could be more explicit. They wrote as follows: "If one wishes to become a Walk-out, there are several methods to be employed. The wish is paramount, for until one willingly relinquishes his body none other of high moral perception may enter. There is a changeover period during which each ego occupies it in turns, but not simultaneously. As the entity who wishes to enter makes the other aware of his loving presence, they will from time to time exchange places while the newcomer becomes acquainted with the bodily mechanism. This may occur at night during sleep, or in daydreams, or during waking periods when one is lonely or wretched. To prepare for a Walk-in, first surround oneself with the golden protective light. Then, as one begins to feel the presence of another, he may invite him in by taking leave of the body for short periods. The best time for this is while lying in bed or on the floor, so that no injury would result from a brief period of unconsciousness while the entity slips into the vacated mind. To ensure that the right entity, or one on the same wavelength, is entering, one should remember that this feeling of 'rightness' is the real test. If he feels relaxed and comfortable, with no sense of panic or remorse, it is satisfactory to proceed with the tentative experiment, for it need not be final until one has said in so many words, 'I will go now, and leave all in your hands.' Then he will rest for a time, before opening his spiritual eyes to the spirit plane."

The same day that the Guides typed this message, on August 23, 1978, an article in the Washington *Post* reported as follows: "Suicides among young Americans have tripled in the last twenty years. About 5,000 Americans between the ages of fifteen and twenty-four take their lives every year. The phenomenon has affected a startling cross-section of youth from all social, economic, and racial backgrounds."

If the Guides are correct, then surely the method they describe is a more ennobling way to withdraw from an intolerable situation than to quench the flame of life and incur karmic penalty through suicide.

The Guides phrased it like this: "Walk-ins are helping others find their way to self-understanding, quietly assisting them to look within, to find that core within self from which all knowledge flows. They are at work in a variety of ways, as physicists, truckers, teachers, scholars, writers, and housewives, for until they are freed of tasks undertaken by the original owners of the bodies, they will not advance their own work, which is that of trying to bring peace and understanding between peoples.

"Those who would contemplate suicide might better give thought to permitting these superior souls to use their bodies, and let them take over during sleep or sickness, withdrawing into spirit to rest for a time and reassess their own goals.

"Why destroy a usable body, when it will serve a laudable purpose for another?"

Why, indeed!

CHAPTER II

This New Age

The Piscean Age ushered in by Jesus Christ two thousand years ago brought the electrifying message that all men are brothers, equally beloved by their Creator. Because the fish represents the Piscean sign of the zodiac, early Christians used drawings of fishes to signify conversion and identify themselves to each other.

The water bearer is the symbol of the Aquarian Age that our planet is now entering, and the Guides say that water will cover many areas of our present continents after the shift of the earth on its axis, even as other land masses emerge from the seas. They will have a great deal more to say about this dramatic event later in the book.

The earth is in constant evolution, and science has been our reigning king since the Industrial

Revolution, bringing untold technological advances to mankind. The next evolution of our planet will be mental, and Walk-ins are said to be returning by the thousands to speed the advent of an improved race, able to cope with the earth changes ahead. If the information given to me is accurate, our ever-expanding network of communications may then become outmoded. Many Walk-ins are able to communicate directly with each other through mental telepathy, while also tuning into the Group Minds of Brotherhoods, and as mankind evolves in the New Age eventually everyone will be able to tap into this vast reservoir of knowledge, creating a dramatically different world society.

For some it will be a rocky road, because if others can read our thoughts it will be impossible to lie or cheat without discovery. No one will be able to keep a secret and no crimes will go unsolved. One's motivation must of necessity be pure, and although the telepathic age will not come to full fruition in our present lifetime, a thousand years hence a new breed of people may shake their heads in wonder at the dishonesty and concealment of our era.

The Guides say of this enchanted road: "The New Age has begun, but will not be fully recognized as such until the shift of the axis has eradicated some of the evils of the present age. The earth will be swept clean of the beastliness and cupidity that now surrounds us, and will see the flowering of a civilization in which the best of man's instincts are given full range. Those times will see communication by mental rather than vocal or pictorial processes, so that evil is suppressed to a marked degree; for thoughts are things—make no mistake about it. 'Think no evil' is as important as 'Speak no evil,' or 'Hear no evil.' With thought transference from mind to mind, today's elaborate systems of communication will be less needed. Why have satellites to spy on another's doings when it is possible to read his mind at a distance and forestall his evil intents? There will be little motivation for greed, since love of others instills a wish to share.

"This New Age is the millennium of which the Bible speaks, when all of mankind are brothers without regard to race, sex, or creed. School systems will be drastically altered, for by tapping directly into the minds of others, one may secure the information he requires, without attending classrooms for twelve or sixteen years. The learning process will be speeded up, because books can be read almost at a glance, and the material contained therein absorbed through mental osmosis. It will be a lively and interesting time, and many of those souls who yearn for perfection will find it easier to achieve and will not thereafter need to return to physical body again and again to confront the same temptations of avarice, envy, and lust."

Inasmuch as my new Walk-in friend, Laura, has made tantalizing references to Brotherhoods and Group Minds, I asked the Guides to elaborate. They replied that many Brotherhoods are already in existence, each with a Group Mind into which members can tap, and that the memberships are composed of both discarnates and incarnates, including Walk-ins.

"They form a close-knit group, with from fifty to several hundred incarnates in each Brotherhood," the Guides said. "These Brotherhoods specialize in different fields, so that while one may be occupied with mathematical calculations or harmonic vibrations, others will be engaged in managerial or counseling services, intelligence gathering, or science. So attuned are they to the universe and to each other that those at a distance with like vibrations are able to tune into their Group Minds through mental telepathy for guidance and solution to problems."

After a short time in physical body, Walk-ins are apparently made aware of these Brotherhoods, and when they develop their full potential they need pause only momentarily to tune into the particular Group Mind on which they wish to draw for information. One of the tasks for experienced Walk-ins is seeking out and assisting newly arrived Walk-ins until they grasp their newfound abilities. Laura, having so recently discovered her own status, has such a helper, a wise old lady who is a member of a Brotherhood. One day on the telephone I plied this lady with questions, which she readily answered, and after she handed the receiver to Laura, I asked her to explain Group Mind. Laura's helper heard my query, and replied, "Tell Ruth the responses I have just been giving her came from Group Mind."

The Guides say of this phenomenon: "Western

peoples are only recently beginning to utilize this vast reservoir of information, because until one's mind is opened to the potential of harmonic minds working in unison toward a common goal, the door is closed. Many Easterners for thousands of years have known of this glorious fountain of knowledge, and have made use of it. In this respect America is far behind many regions of the world, even Russia, and the Soviets are moving more rapidly than the United States to tap into the wealth from this source."

Laura came to visit me and sat in on one of my morning sessions when I asked the Guides for still more clarification of Brotherhoods and Group Mind. After greeting our visitor, they wrote: "As to Group Minds, they are a part of the Brotherhoods, composed both of discarnates and incarnates. They are available to those on like wavelengths and to those who can so fine-tune their vibrations as to tap into them. Some are of the type to which Miriam (Laura's helper) belongs, eager to free men's minds from the barnacles of earth living, while others have such specific purposes as solving equations, bringing inventive forces into play, and working with nations and individuals for the common good. There is a federation of Serving Brotherhoods, worldwide in its reach, which is made up of sixty Brotherhoods, symbolically termed the White Feather, the Gold Circle, the Overall Mind, the Spiral, and others too numerous for naming. Each has a Group Mind that is ordinarily available only to those who have taken the pledge of selflessness, love, and service.

As these Group Minds delve into problems presented to them, the consensus feeds out almost as rapidly as the questions mentally feed in. Man's puny computers are as children's toys compared with this massive operation, which is always at work with the speed of thought itself. We will tell you more about Group Mind and Brotherhoods at a later time. Laura will become an active member of one of them within the next six months or so, and her alteration of living style will occur at about the same time."

This would seem to suggest that my new friend Laura has just about completed the tasks she inherited from her predecessor in that body, and is ready to go forward to her own projects.

Another sign of the New Age now dawning is the back-to-the-earth movement. A new breed of young people is determined that rather than raping Planet Earth, we should be working in harmony with its energies. Many people are returning to natural things, using herbal remedies rather than chemical products, and practicing holistic medicine. They insist on food that is grown without harmful pesticides, talk to their plants, sing to their gardens, and employ only natural fertilizers. They throng the health-food stores, bake their own bread, give birth to babies at home without an anesthetic, and trek to meditation centers and communes in the United States, Europe, India, and elsewhere throughout the world to learn how to deal with universal energies.

Walk-ins are quietly encouraging this return to self-reliance, suggesting that instead of pressuring government to provide ever more services, we should rely on ourselves and each other, as our rugged forefathers did. The emphasis is on individual effort, rather than mass society, and on freedom of choice. Many Walk-ins now occupy the bodies of the so-called war babies of the 1940s and 1950s who have reached adulthood and are crowding today's work force. These Walk-ins realize that because the population explosion has now abated, there will be insufficient workers to support the social security system as now constituted, when they reach retirement age. Thus they are suggesting that young people learn do-it-yourself skills that can be bartered with each other, since they will probably be unable to live on social security payments. California's Proposition 13, which has sparked similar drives throughout the country, is a cry for fewer Big Brother services and less waste, saying in effect, "Let's do it ourselves. Let's clean up our welfare rolls. Let's go back to the teaching of basics in education and forget the frills. Let's stop paving the earth with more highways and more parking lots for more gas-guzzling automobiles. Let's learn to cut our own firewood and grow our own food."

Inasmuch as many Walk-ins are leading the way toward this resurgence of self-reliance, I asked the Guides if any of our current political leaders are Walk-ins, and they replied: "In the U.S. government there are some in reasonably high places and in intelligence-gathering circles, but successful politicians are less likely to give way to a replacement than are those who have become discouraged and heartsick. A few have attained political power since becoming Walk-ins but at present there is not an abundance of them in the higher echelons."

I wondered if Walk-ins are prevalent in Russia today, and they replied in the affirmative, saying: "The time is close at hand when many Russian citizens will be making way for Walk-ins, feeling that this is the most effective way they can be of service in the difficult two decades ahead. There are already a considerable number in the Soviet Union, and their work is crucial to the advancement of that people toward mental and spiritual freedom. It will take time, but they are planting the seeds for a new spirit in that closed society. In China, too, there are Walk-ins, and it is easier to pinpoint them there because of the radical alteration in philosophy of that government within the past two years. But none of these must be individually identified, or their opportunities would be destroyed."

My Walk-in friends say that in the New Age this warring planet will become unified, with one government, one language, and one currency. They stress that this does not signify communism or socialism, but a new way of life that will evolve from an inner awakening to the basic laws of interaction. Many of these cosmic laws are so simple that one needs only try them to prove their workability: Whatever we give to life returns to us three-fold; if we love and encourage others, believing in them, they will automatically believe in us; when we help others we should keep it a

secret, expecting no reward; if wronged by another, we should bless him in our heart and give
him the freedom to make mistakes as he seeks his
own pathway, remembering the Biblical injunc-
tion, "Judge not, lest ye be judged"; whatever
bread you cast upon the waters will return to you
in kind. If you steal you will be stolen from. If you
hate, you will be hated. When you give help, you
will receive help. Above all, learn to rely on your
own intuition. It is the spark of God within us.

The Brotherhoods are playing an active part in
disseminating these laws of interaction. The Guides
say of them: "We here (in spirit) are regularly in
touch with these groups, and are helped by them
as they are by us. At the close of this century the
world will be in utter turmoil, and those still in
flesh who have participated in the work of the
Brotherhoods and other spiritual centers will be of
vast and incomprehensible authority to aid in the
restoration of civilian habitation and land usage
after the shift of the axis. They will tap unforeseen
resources to feed the hungry, house and clothe
them. Fear is pointless, because from the ashes of
that debacle will arise a greater society, with a harmony never before seen on Planet Earth. Truth will
shine forth, and those who survive in flesh will
reach new heights of camaraderie and peace."

The Guides say that many spirit entities are
available to help release those who wish to avoid
the turmoil of the late 1990s by becoming Walk-
outs. The Walk-ins then in physical body "will find
peaceful enclaves for those who want to live out
their earthly existence, and they are already

trying to bring a modicum of intelligence to those groping in the dark for solutions to the world's ills.

"These will be a strenuous two decades ahead for Mother Earth," they continued, "and many will wish that they had not chosen this particular time for rebirth into flesh. However, they need have no fear of ultimate survival, because the soul is imperishable, and the good that comes of standing up to stresses and helping others will forward their soul's progress. Some humans will survive, and others will find themselves without bodies as the destruction occurs, but all will have immortality. The preparation is in an inner state of altered consciousness, and erasing fear is a primary task of Walk-ins in a position to prepare others for the swift alteration of the earth's surface. Serenity is the keyword, and this state of mind is achieved by loving others, or at least sending them on their way with a blessing. Do that which is good, and nothing will rebound to evil."

Walk-ins sounded like such nice people that I finally mustered sufficient courage to ask the Guides if I am one. After all, my life took a rather abrupt turning when I gave up my syndicated political column to write books on psychic matters. But my unseen pen pals are not given to flattery.

"No, you are not a Walk-in," they bluntly replied. After a moment's pause, they added: "But one day you may decide to make way for a Walk-in. Until then, do that which you came into this earth to do. We'll help."

CHAPTER III

Is This for Real?

After completing the first two chapters of this book, I reread them and then began to panic. I have a horror of misleading others in my own quest for universal truth. How could I know for sure that there actually are Walk-ins? Dared I lend my respected by-line to such a far-out theme if I lacked proof of it?

As a seasoned newspaper writer, I have always been a skeptic, and like Thomas in the New Testament (John 20:24) I would probably have insisted on inspecting the print of the nails before believing that Christ had risen from the tomb.

Filled with sudden doubts, I spent some anguished hours before the next day's session with the Guides, whom I have grown to trust simply because of their time-tested veracity and the accuracy of their predictions. Therefore, before beginning the morning meditation, I typed these questions: "Is all this about Walk-ins really true, or am I being taken in? Will it make me sound ridiculous?"

Later, as I rested my fingers lightly on the typewriter keys, the Guides firmly capitalized these words: "WHAT WE TELL YOU IS TRUTH." Only a brief pause ensued before they continued: "What is so strange about a Walk-in with good motivation taking over by invitation an unwanted body, when the world is aware that evil entities can enter occupied bodies and cause untold suffering? Outstanding psychiatrists have examined, worked with, and written about many much cases in which multiple egos war for possession of an inhabited body. Do you think that evil is more powerful than good? Do you believe that a high-minded soul has less capability than a mischievous or unethical one to enter the body of another?

"There is so much of which puny man is unaware! He uses only five percent of his mind. He ordinarily recognizes nothing beyond his five physical senses; yet the power of the human mind is scarcely tapped. Keep on with the book, and help to bring some enlightenment to those about you. We are trying to help those in flesh to understand the greater world of spirit. Those now in physical body will one day be among us here, and the preparation while there will shorten their learning time on this side."

Somewhat abashed, I recalled Christ's admonition to his doubting disciple: "Thomas, because thou hast seen me, thou hast believed. Blessed are they that have not seen, and yet have believed." Should I, who have been privileged to speak with several persons identified to me as Walk-ins, refuse to share the experience with others, and perhaps to help them understand themselves or their neighbors?

It seemed a good time to ask the Guides to explain this mysterious process of automatic writing by which they communicate through me. Ever willing to instruct, they wrote: "We would begin by saying that as you take this writing each morning, it flows through your subconscious and into your fingertips as if it were all one process. We are not pressing the typing keys, as that is done automatically by you when triggered by your mind. The words are put into that mind by us as we sense the awakening of the subconscious, which is often a slumbering giant. You are most receptive when in the so-called alpha state, an altered state of consciousness that can be measured on an electroencephalograph. This is a relaxed, passive state in which you are scarcely aware of that which flows into and out of the mind, and is most often achieved during meditation, or shortly before one drifts into or out of sleep. In this state, the triggering device of mind-to-fingertips, through your years of touch-typing, is uninterrupted. This is what the subconscious does best—reacts automatically to stimuli through long habit. Then, as we offer the incentive, the mind and fingers respond automatically. It is a system easy to learn and to acquire if one is a touch-typist. Otherwise, the two-finger typing system would be more difficult to manage; but since nearly all are able to write with a pencil, that too is automatically controlled without a whole new learning process." (Most automatic writing begins with the pencil, as mine did.)

Continuing their discussion, the Guides wrote: "As to the Ouija board, anyone capable of getting his own will out of the way for a short time is able to receive messages through the pointer, as it gently glides with fingertip control. This and the planchette are the easiest beginner's tools for taking thoughts from those who are disembodied spirits, and they are harmless unless one is seeking only amusement or self-gratification, in which event discarnates without spiritual orientation will gladly frolic and play, and even attempt practical jokes to even the score. Best not to dabble in Ouija and planchette unless determined to seek spiritual advancement, for otherwise they become dangerous toys. It is the same with table-tipping, if done at parties for the amusement and stupefaction of those who are laughing and drinking. These are simple methods for attuning to those who have passed on, and sometimes are very rewarding. But beware of the fools at play, both in and out of the body."

Amused at their expressive last sentence, and somewhat reassured, I asked if Walk-outs and Walk-ins should be described as kindred souls. The Guides replied that the replacing soul is generally on the same wavelength with the Walk-out, although they were not necessarily associated in past incarnations.

"They are kindred," they wrote, "in the sense that they are able to communicate readily with each other on the vibratory level, and they are in touch with each other for a time before the final substitution. They are both ones who wish to help others, although the way they go about it is often dissimilar. Those on this side assist in the substitution, and some in the spirit state are engaged in this as their principal task, while others have different tasks, as we have told you. They quiet the unease of the departing one, helping him to adjust to the change into spirit once he is here, and there are some spirits who work with him while he is preparing to become a Walk-out, sensing his moods and instilling confidence in him. Understand, there is no pressure whatsoever for a person to become a Walk-out. It is entirely his choice, freely made, and although he may not necessarily realize it, his wishing for a long period of rest from worldly cares helps prepare the way for a Walk-in."

While writing this chapter, one of my new friends introduced me to the writings of Tuesday Lobsang Rampa, who employs the term "body change" rather than Walk-in. Rampa says of himself that in a previous Tibetan incarnation he entered Chakpori Lamasery in Lhasa as a *chela,* or novice, at the age of seven, and after intensive training as a priest-surgeon became a lama, and finally an abbot; that he was sent to the University of Chungking in China to study American methods of medicine and surgery as well as the Chinese system, survived starvation and torture at the hands of the Japanese during World War II, and eventually died. Almost immediately thereafter, he writes, he entered the body of a consenting adult Englishman who withdrew on June 13, 1949, leaving Rampa the Occidental body that he needed to carry on his medical work.

In *The Rampa Story,* a Bantam paperback, he declares, "We must bring to the knowledge of many the truth that one ego can depart his body voluntarily and permit another ego to take over and reanimate the vacated body." He also wrote, "We would have people know how a body may be discarded like an old robe for which the wearer has no further use, and passed on to another who needs such a body for some special purpose."

In *Chapters of Life,* another of his books, Rampa writes: "People fear that which they do not understand, and so if it is said that a person has changed bodies with another, then he is automatically the subject of much persecution. But it is necessary that there be incidents of changing bodies to bring it into the public consciousness."

My Walk-in friends say that critics in England and West Germany have derisively hooted Rampa, and that he now writes in bitterness. Inasmuch as they also told me that Walk-ins should not publicly reveal their changed status, I asked the Guides if Rampa's problems stem from his assertion that he, a Tibetan lama, now occupies the body of a departed Englishman. This is their reply: "Rampa is not being persecuted for revealing that he is a Walk-In. The time was right for this disclosure, and he proceeded according to plan. However, he soon will be coming over here for further instructions, and will no doubt regret some of his later writings. Not for us to judge."

Since Rampa consistently uses the term "body change," and I had never heard the term Walk-in until receiving the letter from Laura, I asked her how the latter term originated. I was told that it is a loose translation of the Sanskrit word *avesha*, as used in Hindu scriptures, and of *boddhisattva*, as found in Buddhist literature, and that those entering the bodies of willing American adults have begun using the term "Walk-in" only within the past few years.

Laura, as well as the Guides, stressed that help from discarnates is required to make the substitution of one entity for another. I therefore asked my unseen pen pals if they could be more specific in describing how these discarnates effect the changeover, and they replied: "They arrange receptive channels and vibratory levels, and tune into the receptive one to help arrange a peaceful substitution." Then, in their inimitable manner of expression, they continued: "They are insurance policies, so to speak, against a takeover by the wrong entity or by one whose vibrations are of a different wavelength than the one who wishes to retire from his body. Theirs is a skilled operation, as you might phrase it. They are specialists in their work, and highly evolved."

The Guides said that Walk-ins who enter adult bodies are able, "through intuition and fresh recollections of akashic records, to get on more rapidly with tasks that require help from this side." Since they are not blanking out that knowledge through the process of birth and childhood, "they are more readily available for projects needed to instill mankind with greater awareness and seeking within.

"They are to be lauded for this unselfish work," they continued, "for it is not an easy task they have set themselves. They take on another's problems, and even his bodily ills, and while aiding others are not prepared to accept praise or acclaim. They work in secrecy for the good of mankind, and are modest, striving souls who suffer as they see the course of present events."

Perhaps I was mentally picturing Walk-ins as godlike individuals without flaws, because on another day the Guides wrote: "They are superior souls in that they have completed a sufficient number of commendable previous lifetimes to enable them to skip the birth process, but they are not perfected souls or they would not return in the guise of human beings. They have faults to overcome, even as you or we do, and they realize this, for they often take on menial tasks to finish the work of the Walk-outs, and they do it unstintingly and uncomplainingly, in the realization that they are also working out entangling karma of their own. They wish to overcome in one or more lifetimes all that has previously blemished their earthly records, for they are fully aware that the state of bliss is the spirit kingdom and reunion with the Creative Force of the universe. Many of them will not need to spend lifetime after lifetime going from one body to another, because if they are successful in one or more such cycles they will be able to go and come as the exalted ones." This presumably referred to certain perfected beings, the avatars in Eastern religions who can reportedly materialize at will before their disciples, just as Jesus Christ was seen by various groups after relinquishing his physical body.

Most Walk-ins zealously guard the secret of their altered identity, because people tend to fear what they consider supernatural. If one among them claimed to be occupying a body in which another had been born, he would probably be shunned or made the butt of crude jokes. If a mother, happily noting the improvement in an adult offspring, were informed that in fact the child to whom she had given birth had withdrawn, and that a stranger now occupied that body, she would needlessly grieve. Her pride in the metamorphosis of that individual would diminish, and in its place would be the negative qualities of confusion, guilt, and resentment.

No Walk-in wishes to embroil himself in controversy, or to bring sadness and regret to family members who have begun to notice positive changes in one among them. The status does not matter nearly as much as the projects to be undertaken. The work of Walk-ins is at the mental level, inspiring others to seek inner awareness and rely on their intuition.

With their own intuitive knowledge they recognize what sages have been teaching for thou-

sands of years: There is no death. There are no
miracles, but simply the proper utilization of life
energies that function according to cosmic law.
Life cannot be bargained with. If one wants something of life he must first give selflessly to it. The
way of soul evolution is equally open to all,
whether rich or poor. All of us have full freedom
of choice as to what we will do with this life, how
we will do it, and when we will do it.

Time is infinite, and as each of us began as
sparks from our Creator, so our ultimate goal is
reunion with Him. We are surrounded by life
energies and healing forces that we can learn to
use by moving with the Universal Flow and ac-
cepting our occasional setbacks with good grace.
That is what this book is all about. There is no
such thing as a "bad" experience, but only opportunities to learn and grow in inner understanding.
As the Guides succinctly phrase it: "Our stum-
bling blocks are stepping stones."

CHAPTER IV

In Ages Past

The Guides report that Walk-ins are now returning to earth in greater numbers than at any time since shortly before the destruction of Atlantis, the legendary land whose technologically evolved civilization so chillingly parallels that of America today. Then, as now, they felt the urgent need to preserve what was best, to resettle those who wished to survive in physical body, and to eradicate the fear of death by teaching that life is eternal.

"Walk-ins of ages past have performed many exciting projects to benefit the human race," the Guides wrote one morning. "Those in Atlantis were instrumental in secreting the records in safe places in the Yucatan and Egypt. Through inner awareness they realized that the end of the island kingdom was nearing. They therefore made herculean efforts to rescue the remnants of that civilization, so that in future eras the records would be discovered, as they will be after the shift of the axis at the end of this century. In the present era they are rushing back to forestall the total destruction of man's present knowledge of science and industry, and to awaken his awareness of the inner self and the greater life beyond the grave."

At another session my unseen friends said that today's Walk-ins are working to prepare us for the shift of the axis, which is inevitable, and are valiantly trying to prevent World War III, which is not inevitable if men will change their attitudes. "The ways they go about it are varied," they wrote, "but they are all synonymous. Some work through Brotherhoods and meditate together for the peace of the world. Others are driving taxis, working in stores, factories, offices, and other types of everyday jobs, seeking to spread the feelings of brotherhood, fellowship, and love. To do this, they engage in conversation with their fellow workers, dropping seeds of wisdom through casual remarks that are more apt to be heeded when coming from an equal than from a preacher or boss. In times past Walk-ins have led mankind to discoveries of ancient artifacts and to the preservation of written documents. They have held conclaves with far-sighted individuals in order to prevent wars, settle boundary disputes, and teach others how to tune into the wisdom of the ages through telepathy and inner knowing."

Eager to know more about their specific accomplishments in previous eras, I prodded the Guides for details, and they wrote: "In the days of the Roman Empire there were many Walk-ins who sought to rescue from invaders precious manuscripts, and also precious minds that would otherwise have been quenched. In Grecian times they held forth against Roman invaders, protecting the Acropolis and other fine buildings, and the records of high accomplishments. This has ever been a task for Walk-ins, to preserve the best of each civilization so that all is not lost to succeeding generations. In the Middle Ages some were copyists who wrote down and preserved texts. In Babylonian times they were there to lead the wandering tribes and help them find their way out of captivity. The Mayans of Central America had Walk-ins who led them into the rain forests and away from conquering Spaniards.

"Walk-ins were among the Essenes at Qumram, secreting the [Dead Sea] scrolls in sealed vases in virtually inaccessible caves and caverns, and not all of these scrolls have yet been unearthed. Among the Jewish zealots at Masada were several Walk-ins who, during that prolonged siege by Roman soldiers, took over the adult bodies of some who wished to avoid starvation. They were defending the truth of One God against the pagan invaders who would destroy the Jewish worship. The Walk-ins were there to the last [when the Dead Sea fortress finally fell], not persuading others to die, but explaining how they themselves had died and then returned to the bodies they were inhabiting. They thus gave tremendous courage and assurance to the loyal defenders of truth."

Ever since my first glimpse of the Dead Sea area many years ago, I have been irresistibly drawn to it, returning there again and again, as if it had cast a spell on me. I consequently asked the Guides if they would supply more information about ancient happenings there, and they wrote: "Four Walk-ins were at Sodom and Gomorrah, in the latter days when the cities were evil; two in each city. The cities were headed for destruction, even as much of America is today, and the Walk-ins tried desperately to turn the people from evildoing. Had there been hundreds of Walk-ins there, it might have been possible to avert the disaster, but the opportunity was lacking, because those who enjoy evil ways are not likely to surrender their bodies to others who would occupy them for beneficial purposes.

"Now as to World War III, which lies ahead, the situation is similar. Were there millions of Walk-ins working in unison, that catastrophe could perhaps be prevented, but in this present age of prosperity, how many luxury lovers are likely to say to a discarnate, 'Take my place. I'm ready to go on.' Those who do not believe in eternal life or in salvation for the soul are enjoying the present age like heady wine, for they earn more than their labors justify, and are bent on pleasure and wealth. It will ever be thus, as long as we have people in authority who encourage wasteful ways, freely supporting those who prefer welfare to work, and giving little thought to those laboring under the yoke of heavy taxation in order to support the wastrels. If those too indolent to support themselves would be willing to surrender their physical bodies to Walk-ins, so many could enter that the nuclear war of the late 1980s might yet be averted, but this is unlikely to occur."

In rereading this segment from the Guides, I thought of Lot's wife, who, according to the Biblical account (Genesis 19:17; 26), was turned to a pillar of salt for disobeying instructions not to look back at the destruction of Sodom. Before beginning the next day's session, I smilingly remarked that Lot's wife must not have been one of the Walk-ins, since they sound so all-wise, and the Guides wrote: "Lot was a Walk-in, but his wife was not: nor would she have been his choice as a mate. Lot's was a body that he entered in middle years, and he had to finish what that body had begun under previous ownership. Thus he fulfilled his mission and has gone on to exalted status. Lot's two daughters (who escaped with him) were not Walk-ins, but the three other Walk-ins whom we have previously mentioned stayed in the idolatrous cities to the end in order to help others, at the final moments, to see the light and mend their ways. Lot was selected to lead out those who would go. So few of them, alas."

Aware of the Biblical account of the Lord's destruction of the two cities through "brimstone and fire," I asked what actually transpired and my unseen pen pals wrote, "The fire and brimstone were the results of an atomic explosion set off, not by man, but by forces within the earth and above.

It was a nuclear type, with radiation, but did not affect as many as it would have if the area were heavily populated. It was sufficient, however, for the two cities to be inundated by the Dead Sea, where remnants of that civilization will one day be unearthed. There were also nuclear explosions in Atlantis, set off by man, which hastened the demise of that island kingdom. Nothing is new under the sun, and the bombs dropped at Hiroshima and Nagasaki were simply descendents of earlier explosions of like magnitude. Unless mankind radically alters its approach, many will be slaughtered through no fault of their own in the next decade. It is ever thus with wars, and the onus is on those who take the offensive into their hands, and step by step lead their nation along the war path."

The Guides' comments on the valiant Jews at Masada, and their dire predictions for World War III turned my thoughts toward the Holocaust in Germany during World War II, and after I asked the Guides about that dreadful stain on history, they wrote: "Some of those who prevented others from going to Hitler's gas chambers by sacrificing their own lives were Walk-ins, and some were simply high-minded souls who had grown to understand the meaning of 'love one another,' and many of these became so exalted through their sacrifice that they need never return to physical body. There are Walk-ins in Germany today to ensure that a threatening new rise of Nazism will die aborning. Never again will the world see such slaughter of innocent Jews."

Inasmuch as the Guides had, within that single paragraph, looked both backward in time and forward into the future, I wondered how they dared speak with such seeming authority. Apparently taking no offense at my doubting-Thomas questioning, they explained: "The way we work is to tap into the akashic records for past events, and see farther than you earthlings into the future. Thus, we have a far wider range of vision than do those in physical form. The Walk-ins are also able to tap into this reservoir of knowledge through telepathy and inward seeing."

They then reminded me of their comparison, in *The World Before,* of a canoe to an airplane. They said that we humans, as we paddle along, see only as far as the next bend in a winding river, totally oblivious to any hazards that we may encounter ahead, whereas those in spirit are like the pilot of an airplane overhead, who not only sees the course our canoe has already traveled, but with the wider range of vision from above, the path that lies beyond.

Whenever I have specific questions for the Guides, I type them before my morning meditation, and I had asked several times about our own American past before they finally indulged my curiosity, writing: "As to the discovery of America, Christopher Columbus himself was a Walk-in who recalled times when the truth of a global earth was well known to all men. He had been an Atlantean during its finest era, when earthlings circumnavigated the earth in ships and planes propelled by the giant Crystal. In returning to the body of an adult seaman, Columbus felt the need again to enlighten humanity of the vast reaches beyond its known shores. Having not been in physical body since before Atlantis was destroyed, he did not at first recognize that the islands where he landed [in the West Indies] were undiscovered land, because the earth's surface had vastly altered since Atlantean days. Columbus was a farsighted Atlantean who wished to help the earthlings open their horizons and stretch out to understand the universe. He is here now, in spirit, and happy to have this fact told."

Soon after that revelation, the Guides began the morning session in chatty fashion, declaring: "We will tell you of the early Americans who settled a new land. Some were leaders of those excursions, and surely you realize that William Penn (1644–1718) was a Walk-in! He was an inestimable soul who founded a new colony [Pennsylvania] with religious freedom for all in the name of peace and brotherly love. There were other Walk-ins among the pioneers in those early days, and we will not attempt to name them now, but so many persecuted people needed reassurance that there was a large influx of Walk-ins to lead them out of the narrow bigotry of Europe and into the freedom of a new land. The American Indians are a psychic race, because of their closeness to nature, and many of them recognized these superior beings, such as Penn, and sensed their love, while some other white men confused and angered them by their selfishness and greed.

"America," they continued, "had a number of

outstanding Walk-ins at its birth as a republic. Not all of those noble fighters for freedom were Walk-ins, by any means, but there was a sufficient group of them that through their influence freedom was won, and among the signers of the Declaration of Independence were three Walk-ins. Benjamin Franklin, of course, was one of them."

Shortly after naming the illustrious Quaker, William Penn, the Guides unexpectedly identified John Greenleaf Whittier as a Walk-in. Since I chiefly associated the New England poet with "Snow-Bound," I turned to the *Encyclopaedia Britannica* and learned that he too was a Quaker, and that his biographies do indeed seem to fulfill the qualifications for Walk-out and Walk-in as outlined by the Guides and my new friends. He was a victim of unrequited love, and never married. At the age of twenty-four he became seriously ill, shortly after the death of his father forced the budding poet to give up his publishing job and return to run the family farm near Haverhill, Massachusetts. Thus, lacking close personal ties and in extremely poor health, it is possible that the original occupant of the body may have withdrawn in favor of the Walk-in who shortly thereafter became remarkably active in the abolitionist movement, supporting antislavery candidates, and writing forceful abolitionist tracts and poetry. Whittier was a member of the electoral college that elected Abraham Lincoln, whom the Guides have also identified as a Walk-in, and throughout his lifetime Whittier was one of the leading advocates of freedom for all peoples. The Guides have frequently stressed the importance that Walk-ins place on individual freedom, even to make one's own mistakes, and the *Britannica* says of Whittier: "An intense hater of tyranny and as deep and strong a lover of freedom as Milton. He was both a dire prophet and a gentle poet."

When I pressed the Guides to name other famous Americans of the past who were Walk-ins, they beguilingly retorted: "We will tell you some who were not. Albert Einstein was not a Walk-in, but he worked so closely with discarnates on this side that the theories he expounded were fed into his mind almost as a computer takes figures from an incarnate. Oliver Wendell Holmes was not, but he was well selected for birth to that family. He had been a Walk-in in a previous incarnation, but was permitted to enter the vehicle (the mother) in his last life in order to develop his talents within that extraordinary family." I asked whether the Oliver Wendell Holmes referred to was the elder, an author and physician, or the son by the same name who became a Supreme Court justice, and the Guides replied: "It was the younger of whom we wrote."

Since Walk-ins seemed always to be aligned with the good guys against the bad, even when on the losing side, as at Masada, I wondered whether there were instances in which Walk-ins had been arrayed on opposing sides in a confrontation. This question posed no problems for my unseen friends, who wrote that this had frequently occurred. "The Walk-ins on each side are there for the same purpose," they explained, "to help those in fear of death and to instill in them understanding of the forces for good within each man. They have played many important roles on battlefields as generals and privates, admirals and sailors, and each in his own way has contributed to the peace of mind and well-being of those who are sent to die in battle. It is all a part of human evolution."

One thing seems certain. A Walk-in who has entered the adult body of another eventually meets death in physical form just like the rest of us. When that occurs, according to my Walk-in friends, several options are open to them. Some may wait years, or even centuries, to reincarnate, even as you and I. Some may return to the greater freedom of the spirit world for only a few days, in order to reassess their mission and to confer directly with other discarnates before entering another adult body or being reborn as an infant. Some who are still farther along the evolutionary path may, upon the death of their own bodies, pass almost directly into those of willing Walk-outs who may be hundreds or even thousands of miles away. Certain highly evolved souls may choose a series of lifetimes and a series of tasks, one immediately following another through a particular period of history, in order to serve the planet in a time of crisis.

Since this information came from sources who are now incarnate, I questioned the Guides closely, and they verified it, but emphasized: "Walk-ins are not required to take several lives in quick succession. They are not required to do anything. No one is. It is up to each individual soul how often he wishes to return to physical being, provided a vehicle is available. No pressure is put on anyone on this side. We select our own tasks, which we feel to be best suited to our various talents and to the lessons we need to learn. Thus, if one were required to do a quick succession of lives it would amount to duress, as it is termed in earthly living. There is no such thing here. We are our own judge and jury. We freely elect to do that which will aid our soul-advancement, or, if we like, we can also choose to waste our opportunities by re-creating fanciful mansions or pleasure haunts. We can waste time here, even as it has been done in physical body. Time is eternal, and there is no push on this side to get on with the work. Those who refuse to aid others here are in the same category as those in physical body who think only of themselves. They lose the opportunity to serve, and by so doing delay endlessly their own bliss, for bliss of the highest order is reunion with the Creator in perfect harmony. Life is a learning process, whether in spirit or physical body. God sent out the sparks, which are ourselves, to experience and to serve. If some wish to defy this cosmic law, thus remaining earthbound, they have only themselves to blame for their unhappiness."

I was somewhat troubled by the assertion that on occasion a Walk-in whose body dies can almost immediately enter that of another adult, since the Guides had earlier indicated that some preparation with a willing Walk-out is necessary before the transition. But my unseen friends said I was overlooking two factors: Help from several discarnates is always required to effect the changeover, and Walk-ins have more highly developed telepathic powers than most of us. Thus they can be alerted to the willingness of another to surrender his body, and can be in mental contact with that person well before their own body expires.

As an example, the Guides cited Tuesday Lobsang Rampa, "who went immediately into the body of an Englishman with whom he had been in intuitive contact before his own death, for he needed an Occidental's cloak, or body, to make use of the Western medicine he had studied, and to combine it with the ancient wisdom of the East, with which he was thoroughly conversant." Then they added: "The Tibetan (the priest-surgeon) died, and almost immediately entered the body of an Englishman who had felt the presence around him for some time and was glad to participate in the experiment. The original owner of that body is satisfied with the way it turned out and has no regrets."

Well, it was nice to know that the Walk-out had no complaints. And I could not help thinking of that Englishman as I walked past a beauty shop the other day and read the sign posted outside: Walk-ins Welcome. A new way of saying "No appointment necessary."

CHAPTER V

Inner Preparation

My unseen friends seem rather single-minded in their insistence that the principal theme of this book should be the preparation of earthlings for the shift of the axis at the end of this century, with the resultant loss by so many of their physical bodies as they pass into the spirit state. The Guides repeatedly have warned that inasmuch as the population will be decimated at that time, our opportunities for reincarnating will be drastically curtailed for perhaps thousands of years while the earth's surviving inhabitants gradually reproduce, and that we should therefore be making the most of our present opportunities for spiritual refinement.

Perhaps I had grown too complacent with their continual exhortation, because one morning the

Guides jarred me with the new thought that this large-scale influx of souls into the next dimension will pose problems for the spirit world as well. "The coming age will be fraught with peril for those who have not prepared themselves for the transformation into pure spirit," they began. "The heavens, as you call them, will be crowded with newly returned souls as seldom before, and their crossover into spirit will be so juxtapositioned as to require great preparation and understanding. This will entail hardship for some and will delay the transformation for others, since the will to survive in physical body is strong in the young and healthy. Thus, it is *now* that these younger ones should be assessing their purpose and acquainting themselves with the proper manner of returning to spirit, strong in faith and pledged to work diligently at the enterprise of serving others."

Another day they continued this thought, writing: "Now as to Walk-ins, they are arriving there [on earth] in increasing numbers to help through the two decades ahead. As time goes on, you will be reading and hearing more about enclaves where those who wish to realize awareness will forgather to meditate and plan for the trying times ahead. The Walk-ins are all around you, and you need only open your eyes and ears to become aware of their good deeds. Now as to the climax: When the shift occurs, the earth will suddenly hesitate in its orbit, and shift to a degree where the oceans will pour onto much of the land, wiping off the stains of mankind. Simultaneously, new lands,

submerged for tens of thousands of years, will rise
to the surface. So many souls will be sent to this
side simultaneously that there will be problems
here in assimilating them, and we are preparing
now to cope with the deluge of newly arriving
souls."

The prospect sounded so alarming that, as previously stated, I was extremely reluctant to write
this book. But the Guides, who see life from a
larger dimension, stilled my complaints, declaring: "So many are discouraged and frightened
about the idea of physical death. But why? It is
no more than the passing from one stage to another: caterpillar to butterfly, blossoms to fruit,
and seeds to flowers. All is continuation, progress,
advancement along the path toward eventual reunion with the Creator. There is no such thing as
death. Rather to be feared is the life one leads
before the transition to a more advanced stage of
being."

The Guides can be as inspirational as an old-
time gospel preacher, and one day they wrote:
"The time for preparing for the next stage in man's
evolution is *now*. What we do today, this month,
this year will have strong bearing on the state of
the world a few years hence. If everyone considered the importance of the moment and the hour,
there would be no cause for worry about the future.
We would be so guided by what is right that there
would then be no wrong. To take each shining
hour as a perfect whole, striving to do our best for
those sixty golden minutes, would so revolutionize
the thinking of mankind that strife would disap-

pear. To establish one's claim to fair treatment is to render fair judgment at all times on others. Forgive readily. Vanquish temptation. Yield only to that which is the perfect song of love. Give unto others that which you would like to receive. Hold each day as a precious epitome of one's entire life. Sing a song of thanksgiving to the Creator, who has peopled this earth with souls whom we have known in past ages. Love and give of self. Be not disheartened by the strifes and rivalries of others. 'To thine own self be true.'

"The future has such possibilities for good that the present course is unnecessarily dividing souls. If all would think of others there would be nothing to dread; yet at the present pace of development it will be impossible to avert the wars that lie ahead. To see that awesome challenge from this side of the portal [the spirit world] is to groan at the unlikelihood of altering the course of events. So many are busily 'getting theirs' and 'looking after Number One' that the bestial side of man's nature is giving vent to horrors unlike that seen in the physical plane since Atlantis was destroyed by man's wilfulness and evil. To alter the course of events it would be necessary for each soul in flesh to think of the betterment and advancement of others as well as himself. Such a simple thing to do! The future is now, if one would only understand the universal laws that govern man's progress. Hearken to this. Today's actions are already the tomorrow for all those who inhabit flesh. The future of America and the world depends for the most part on what their inhabitants are thinking

and doing now. Each passing hour is determining
the progress of each soul from this day forward.
Never forget that as we think, we become. Nothing
was ever more truthfully said. Think good, and
one is good. Think evil, and one destroys himself.
Remember that one rotten apple spoils a barrel,
so beware of associating with those who are rotten."

Rereading this at a later date, I was puzzled by
the warning not to associate with those who are
"rotten." Are the Guides not always preaching
that we should love and help one another? For
that matter, how *can* we be expected to love the
vile rapists, the murderers, the drug pushers and
crooks? I put these questions to the Guides, and
they responded: "The way to regard those who
have soiled the earth by contaminating or harm-
ing others is to wish for them another learning
period, afresh, without recollection of this time
around. [Another incarnation without conscious
memory of this lifetime.] After all, the rest of us
may not at some time have been so good ourselves.
Thus, while not wishing to associate with such a
person in this lifetime, we are able to withhold
judgment by remembering that he also was once
a flawless spark of God, and that by bespotting
and besmirching that image he has destroyed his
opportunities in the present life; but we will hope
that he makes amends in future incarnations, so
that he too will eventually find his way back to
the Creator as a part of the perfect whole. Keep
oneself free from the spoilage, but send along a

prayer that the spoiler will one day atone and mend his ways."

One of the most disheartening aspects of today's culture is the daily headlines about grafters in government, murderers-for-hire, large-scale welfare cheaters, sex orgiasts, and the like. Dishonesty and greed seem to have become a way of life, and when I asked the Guides why the decades of the sixties and seventies seem worse than those in the early part of this century, they replied: "This is the result of a strong influx of souls from Atlantean days, who, in other incarnations, have sought to perpetuate the wrong-doing and evil ways of that island-continent in its degenerate times toward the end of its days. These souls have yet to learn the lesson that each incarnation is a testing period, to improve their opportunities for spiritual advancement. They think of self-aggrandizement and physical ease, rather than of a joyous reunion with their Creator. They were scarred souls in spirit before ever they entered the earth, and were among those who cohabited with animals. [The Guides discussed that sorry chapter of human evolvement in *The World Before*.] To advance, one must put others' desires and well-being on a par with his own. There is no other way! As a consequence, they will backslide when they fail to accept this basic law of the universe. This will become apparent as the earth nears the period of the shift of its axis. For a long time thereafter there will be fewer opportunities to return to physical being, since such opportunities depend on the growth of population, and this will be drastically slowed as fewer survivors offer less vehicles for childbirth."

Another day, in referring to "the depths to which so many humans have sunk in these past few decades since the Atlanteans thronged back to do their mischief," the Guides anticipated my question, by writing: "Why, you will ask, had they not overcome such tendencies during the ages past? Because they strove not, even in the spirit state. Some were war victims who were raging against the establishment that had ended their previous sojourns in the flesh. Others had been so enmeshed in wrongdoing that they had made no attempt to return to the physical state, until the baby boom of World War II provided unusual opportunity. Some had been out of flesh for so long that they had lost all memory of how to behave in a disciplined society. They wanted revenge for past wrongs, or they wanted to feel themselves the victors over those who had been avengers in ages past. How unfortunate that they should have returned in such massive numbers, for society deals with a few malcontents or troublemakers without difficulty, but when millions of them enter physical body during the same period, they despoil all around them."

The Guides continue to stress that any foreboding about the coming shift of the axis is a result of man's inability to conceive that his soul, rather than his physical body, is precious. "Were we to say that *souls* were to be destroyed in some debacle it would be disastrous indeed," they wrote, "but this is not in the foreseeable future. The etheric bodies that are of the soul will not perish. The perfect pattern remains, and when clothed with flesh is less exquisite by far than the pattern from which those bodies are formed. To speak of disaster in the physical sense is therefore of minor import. The soul is indestructible, since it is a part of the Creator and of Creation itself. Take heart, therefore, and determine to shine within one's own orbit, to light the path for others. Those who wish to speed their journey would do well now to look around them and see how to lend a helping hand to others and feel a kinship with all of mankind. The time for beginning is now. This day. This hour. Not to heap benefits on those who refuse to help themselves, but on those who struggle for spiritual goodness, and who are so heavy-laden with problems, or hang-ups, that they are unable to see the light at the end of the tunnel."

Referring to the coming holocaust, the Guides said it will be of such proportions that some now living will wish to withdraw from their physical bodies beforehand, rather than face the turmoil. In that event, they will be permitted to do so without incurring bad karma, because Walk-ins will volunteer to take over their bodies and ease the path for others who wish to remain.

These future Walk-ins are now said to be in the same spirit state as the Guides, but after entering adult physical bodies they will be able to communicate more normally with us earthlings than discarnates can. I asked the Guides to explain the method used by spirits to reach those of us in physical body, and they replied: "We are attuned through something akin to thought waves, although of higher frequency, to some in the earth plane who are on similar frequency levels to our own; and as we wish to send to them, we fine-tune our own frequency to the earth cycle, and hence to that particular wavelength, so that we are in instant rapport with them. As they attune themselves to us through the so-called alpha state, we are able to trigger a response somewhat like a plane touching down to earth, landing, after soaring through the stratosphere. As we touch down, so to speak, we establish contact and meld with the minds of those with whom we are attuned.

"In this way, we project pictures or symbols into their wavelength, and they reproject them as their own, unless they realize what is transpiring, as you do with the automatic writing. Were you not actively aware of this communication, we would be able to give you symbols or thought patterns, and as your personal radar reacted with them, you would assume that they were your own ideas and impressions, rather than having been passed along to you from this side. So it is with many inventors and inspired writers who feel that they are projecting from their own thoughts, but in actuality are receiving those ideas and impressions from spirit beings. Were mankind to realize the full potential, we would be able to influence all human beings in this fashion; yet many are poor receivers, and so unaware of anything beyond their own plane that it is like the locks in some dams, which will not permit fish to rise to the higher level and go upstream to spawn."

The assertion that spirits have implanted many of the ideas that inspire inventors and writers would explain why the U.S. Patent Office frequently receives applications for almost identical inventions at the same time, although the inventors are unknown to each other, and why books on the same subject, that was previously untouched, achieve publication simultaneously. These may not be examples of pirating, as is sometimes charged, but of clear channel "receiving" from discarnates.

The Guides have always discouraged questions about individual choice, stressing that it is a part of our own growing process to make decisions, and I have long since ceased to ask about my own future. Perhaps that is why my unseen friends sounded rather apologetic one morning when they wrote: "In the normal course of events we would not tell you of things to come, since it is better for one to help form his own future through his current actions; but since this will affect all mankind in the flesh, as well as geological locations, it behooves us to prepare those who will be drastically affected by the earth's shifting position.

"Many of those living today will see a time of turbulence and disorder. In the 1980s will come wars of devastating ferocity, which will thwart the good intentions of those who would avert such disgraceful conduct that retards man's spiritual advancement. These wars are being set in motion today by meddling in the internal affairs of other countries and by the mistaken notion that all souls in all races are ready for the same self-discipline and self-government."

After this side-swipe at those who would try to impose democracy on all nations, the Guides sternly continued: "There are those, unfortunately, who feel that by turning man loose he will automatically seek goodness. Alas, many have never exercised self-discipline, and some of the welfare projects of the United States government are examples of the kind of sloppy thinking that believes if man has a full stomach and a roof over his head, he will automatically become docile and willing to serve others. Men differ one from another as thoroughly as one's fingerprints differ from those of every other physical body. Some people are born leaders and others insurrectionists. The work ethic, which came to full flower in the United States of America, was the foundation for the greatest advance of mankind in modern times: The belief that even the rich should work and strive to serve others, unlike England and France, where the nobility used to be encouraged simply to live on the revenues handed down from generation to generation. That was parasitic in the extreme. In America all men were taught to work with mind and hands and sweat of the brow. This Puritan work ethic produced a new race—strong, sturdy, gregarious, and generous in the extreme. But now it is the underclass that threatens to become a parasitic growth on American society. Several generations of some families continue to thrive on welfare, making little effort to contribute, while reaping the benefit of the sweat of others' brows. This will have to cease, although it will probably take the wars of the 1980s to convince the current do-gooders that their noble experiment has failed."

Later, after reading this passage, I told the Guides that they sounded like conservative politicians in a silk-stocking district, but they said that they had stated the simple truth. "In the times ahead," they continued, "man will realize that he is so finite in his earthly form that he will cease to quarrel and fight. He will understand that each of us is a part of another, together making up the whole, and when this realization emerges into man's consciousness after the shift of the axis, such peace will flood the earth as it has yet to know.

"Why quarrel with oneself? Why fight an arm with its hand? This discovery of an age-old truth will revolutionize man's thinking, and set him so far above the animals that a new race of people born after the shift will spread the gospel of man's oneness with each other and with his Creator. Glimmerings of it will begin during the next decade, but the wars will thrust it aside, and hatred will supplant goodness as a way of life. The strivings of the underclasses will foment such strife as the world has not yet seen, but the shift of the axis will cleanse the earth and purify the survivors."

Forty years ago, Edgar Cayce, while in a trance state, predicted that the earth would shift on its axis near the end of this century. In *The World Before* I cited evidence that such an event has occurred several times in prehistoric ages since the formation of the earth from gaseous elements. The Guides, pointing out that we have less than twenty years to prepare for the next such drastic occurrence, wrote: "When we of this dimension see what is to come, it seems only right to relay that information if there is a chance of averting catastrophe. In this instance it is difficult to explain why the earth will shift on its axis, regardless of any thought or deed by those in physical form. We here recognize the laws of nature, as they are termed. They will occur regardless of anything that puny man is able to effect. Yet, how man copes with those problems is exceedingly vital to the effect it will have. The activity of physical man indeed alters many events which here seem inevitable; yet he is powerless in the face of immutable natural laws that are part and parcel of the continuing act of Creation.

"The revolutions of the earth will be slowed in the last years of this century, and then with sudden force the earth will flutter and alter its position, so that some frigid areas will become warm, being more toward the sun, while others will cool in the shade of that gleaming body. Thus will the shift occur despite all that engineers and scientists would do to avert it. This force, already set in motion, is irrevocable, but it is a force for good, since the earth will be cleansed of some who are despoiling it, and waters sweeping over lands will help to dispel the poisonous substances that have been spread upon the earth."

To that last remark, at least, environmentalists can say Amen.

CHAPTER VI

Laura's Story

Perhaps it is time to examine in detail the case of the Walk-in with whom I have become the most conversant. That person, of course, is Laura, a portion of whose letter I have already quoted. One reason why it had not occurred to me that she herself might be a Walk-in was because the first part of her letter, while flattering, sounded like others from numerous fans who say that they have profited by the words of my Guides.

It began like this: "Are you still there? I visited my favorite bookstore yesterday and asked if you had published any books since *The World Before*, which came out two years ago, and they checked in all their lists, including that of forthcoming books, but could find nothing I hadn't read. Are you still writing? You haven't retired, have you?

I sincerely hope not. You owe it to your loyal followers to keep sharing the views and information given you by our unseen friends. You have changed our lives. You have helped us to see why we are here on the planet, where we have been before, and what we are all striving toward. You have painted word pictures to show us graphically what really happens at death, and you have quietly proven to us that in reality there is no death, but only change. Thank you for helping us to rise above the fog and see exactly what our lifetimes are all about."

Then came the part in which she wrote: "Are you looking for ideas for future books? I would like to see what your unseen friends have to say about the role of Walk-ins on the planet."

Highly intrigued, I wrote back to ask where she had heard of Walk-ins, and what I might read on the subject, and she replied: "I do not know of anything written thus far about Walk-ins. What I wrote to you comes from personal knowledge. If you need to know more about the source of my information in this area, ask the Guides and they will tell you."

I did indeed ask the Guides, and when I went to see Laura I learned that at the time of her letter, she merely "knew" that Walk-ins were real, having become convinced that one or more persons whom she had met were Walk-ins, and she was eager to learn more about the subject. She had no idea that my unseen friends would identify Laura herself as a Walk-in, and she found it a rather shattering experience to read what they had written. It was one thing to believe that a friend occupies a body previously belonging to another, but quite another to be told by that friend, then by two discarnates just before my visit, and finally by my Guides, that she too had been in spirit form until twelve months before.

Only after this seeming confirmation of the two previous communications did Laura begin to think seriously about the dramatic change that had occurred in her own personality and outlook a year ago, the feeling of another presence about her at that time, and the definite turning point when she managed to break free from a disastrous marriage.

Laura continued her soul-searching after my departure, and she is permitting me to share portions of her diary jottings in the hope that they may help others to discover their real identities. First recording the foregoing events, she wrote: "Slowly the pictures fell together. I remembered how last year in my tiny, dark apartment in another city, I had felt the presence of others, one in particular who asked to experience being in my body. If I am indeed a Walk-in, I have inherited the memory patterns of the original Laura, because I am told that a Walk-in feels as if there has been no substitution. I had welcomed the entity in my dreary little room, sometimes feeling uncomfortable and asking it to go away, but then allowing it to remain there longer. I asked it for help when I needed it, and offered to help it as well."

At that point, Laura had left her incompatible husband and was living alone. Now the diary con-

tinues: "I was told that the other entity wanted
to experience being me, and it did so briefly now
and then. I would lie completely still, and will this
other entity to become me for a while, and I always
wanted the experience of being able to leave, because leaving the body is such a pleasant sensation. It must be the way death feels, this delicious
and loving warmth, a tingling, a rush, and a
whoosh into a state so lovely. But I could never
quite experience it fully, because in order to experience it at all I had to leave, and although I
fully enjoyed the sensation of departing, I carried
back no memories of where I had been.

"Then it became regular and routine. Each
night at bedtime I would relinquish my claim to
this body, and allow the other entity to enter it
and remain in it all night. My only requirement
was that I be permitted to return to the body by
morning. This went on for several weeks, and it
was during this in-and-out period that I experienced a burning desire to fly to another country
and search out the site of a previous lifetime, of
which I had had occasional vivid flashes."

Laura had read of a community that was said
to be a power center, and since it is not far from
the area she located, in which she believes she
lived several hundred years ago, she checked into
the community without advance reservations. Assigned a bed among strangers, she was feeling
restless, unhappy, and guilty about crashing into
a group uninvited. Now to go on with her own
account of that experience:

"On the night before the full moon, there began

the most painful headache I have ever had, around eight o'clock. I decided to go to bed early. I had chosen not to take painkillers, but to deal with the pain on other levels. Pain wracked this entire body, every inch of it. I can never remember such pain. I felt sick. I no longer cared if I finished the week's seminar, no longer cared about anything, and somewhere a connection was made with higher levels. Some stream of energy connected with the top of my head, as I willed the pain to leave the body and go out into freedom. I fell asleep. Two hours later I awakened, and the pain was gone; but in the morning there began the worst day of the entire week. I could do nothing right. People barked at me. I left without breakfast, and wept much of the day. I was in misery, but a young woman, whom I now believe to be a Walk-in, came up and put her arm around me, asking what was wrong. I said I felt that I did not belong there, and should not have come, but she comforted me and made me feel welcome.

"The next day things straightened out, and a change seemed to have occurred. I began to communicate very, very deeply with others I met. I could look into their eyes and sense their past lives. I could read their feelings. With three or four individuals there was a deep, loving communication, and I sat up until the wee hours of the morning, deeply excited.

"After that, the sailing was smoother. I did not then realize that a substitution [of egos] had occurred during the two hours of that headache. I had no idea. One afternoon after arriving back home, as we sat in the kitchen of my apartment, an elderly woman friend said to me, 'You're a Walk-in and don't know it.' This upset me deeply, because I knew it could not be so. There had been no great change, no great transition. I was still *me*, wasn't I? It also upset me because I respected the friend and knew that she had always told me the truth, unless she made an honest mistake. She said that in the previous life of which I had had glimpses I was also a Walk-in, and I could accept that, but not the present life alteration. She told me to file it away and not worry about it; that I would need to prove it to myself.

"And I continued my life as Laura. But as the weeks passed, my body began to change. I gained weight, lots of it. My friend seemed to understand what was happening to me, but I didn't. I left the past relationship of my marriage behind, wrapped up the little details, and gradually completed those things that had previously seemed insolvable. I also sorted through boxes of material things and gave them away, even my wedding gown. They were all a part of the past, part of a person I no longer was. I had no further need of that person's things. I had new tasks ahead. I moved to a new city.

"Slowly the old Laura began to fade away. In her place there emerged a new Laura filled with greater confidence, insight, maturity, and wisdom. This new person did not need an ego trip. This new Laura operated more efficiently at work, and seemed to be able to inject bits of insight into others, in order to help them help themselves. This new Laura, instead of blundering in a fog, could suddenly think more clearly and logically. This new Laura could do good without proclaiming it, could give of herself as the old Laura had been unable to do, could remain in a flow of energies and work with that flow.

"Is this new Laura the entity who had asked Laura for permission to take over? Am I the one who night after night slept in this body, while allowing Laura to leave it and test her wings in the Greater Freedom? Am I one of those who are now arriving in such great numbers to assist with the spiritualization of the planet? At least I know that I am not the same Laura who wore this body until a year ago. She left me a fine vehicle, a good typewriter, a relatively simple life, and a situation free from major family ties. She made her preparations for divorce, leaving only a few loose ties for me to clear up. She left me the tools and the raw material with which to begin. She left me a satisfactory job, enough money, and a few loving friends. She did well. She exited with honor. The transition was gentle and loving, and she welcomed it. She was a good woman. And now it is time to pick up where she left off, and go on to what I must do with the situation I have inherited."

That completed her diary entry, except for certain portions that I have deleted in order to protect her identity. Laura sensed that one day she would be permitted to recall more memories of the actual transition, and I suggested that if this occurred before the book was finished, she might be willing to share them. Five months after our original contact, Laura obliged with the following:

"More than five years before the actual event, I had acquired a death wish, feeling that I had done all that I could and was at a crossroads. I would not have committed suicide, but if I had become terminally ill, I don't think I would have struggled to survive. I would have accepted my fate without any deep regrets. I had been out of college and married for nearly four years. There were horrible times, as well as a few happy times. My husband would waver between fine good humor and deep depression. I remained with him only because I did not want to face my family with the fact that my marriage had failed. Death would have been a convenient way out.

"At this time, we were about to move again. It was the Vietnam period, and since my husband was required to join the military after college graduation, we seemed to move every year or so. I was a teacher, and every time we moved I had to quit my job, pack up our household, settle down somewhere else, and look for another job. Changing states meant trying to obtain teaching certification in the new state, and finding employment by September each year. Whenever I couldn't find a teaching job, I took an office job. At the time of my death wish, this was happening for the fourth time, and life seemed futile."

Laura's friend Miriam says it was at this period that the former entity made the original decision to leave, but that she was not permitted by discarnates to do so until she had exerted her best effort to resolve the problems of the marriage. Miriam said it was also necessary for the old entity to become aware of the spirit world, so that she could choose more intelligently the right time to leave the body. Laura at this time had never heard of Walk-ins, and she had rejected organized religion. She was also unaware of the theory of reincarnation, but she says that "when my Catholic mother recommended Ruth Montgomery's books on that subject to me, I found myself devouring them, and looking for more.

"All of a sudden, life began to make sense," she continues. "Every bit of material in those books rang true, whereas information from the clergy had always left me with doubts, unanswered questions, and a feeling that I was being treated to myths. My newfound understanding of life suddenly gave me greater freedom, for it helped to fit my entire life into perspective. I began to become aware of the spirit world around us. On a few occasions I was visited by discarnate entities in my room at night, and although I never physically saw them, I knew they were there. One night I felt one take my hand and squeeze it. I began to listen more intently to my intuition, and found that I often avoided danger or delays when I took a different route [to work] that seemed to feel right."

But Laura's marriage did not improve, and she sought counseling to learn how to handle the problems without letting them destroy her self-confidence. She says of this period: "I learned how to go about my business and do the best I could, without feeling responsible for the radical ups and downs of my husband's moods. I did all I knew how to help him and to stabilize the marriage, but when I could do no more it was time to leave."

Laura gave up her right to a mutually owned property in order to avoid further entanglements, because she had begun to realize that freedom meant more to her than money or possessions. To secure that freedom she relinquished so much of the joint assets that she was left with virtually nothing, but on the day that the final divorce papers were signed, a distant relative died and unexpectedly left her three times what she had given up. This seemed to verify the ancient teaching that whatever we do for others will return to us threefold.

During the period before the divorce, while clearing up the entanglements, Laura moved to the small, dark apartment previously mentioned, and "I had discarnate friends in that apartment right from the beginning," she says. Night after night she sensed the presence of several, but of one in particular who seemed to be studying her while she showered, and hovering over her as she slept. She has already described for us how she finally permitted the entity to occupy her body during sleep, while she seemed to move out to another dimension. When the divorce decree became final, she took a leave of absence from work to find the spot she had known as "home" in a previous lifetime; and after discovering it to her own inner satisfaction, she visited the community where the substitution of egos apparently became final. Now, after more than a year, she has finally begun to "see" that setting from the discarnate point of view. In other words, through the eyes of the "new" Laura, whom she has become since taking over the body of the girl with the death wish.

"The transition team," she says, "seemed to be headed by a wise one, an old soul of highest mind, of deep love and understanding and kindness. I stayed at the foot of the bed, surrounded by others, as he worked at the head of the bed with his discarnate hands. The girl occupying the body lay on the bed. The headache bothered her terribly, and she felt sick and disinterested in whether she lived. As was her custom when she had a headache, she pictured it as a physical mass, willing it to leave through the top of her head and go out into freedom. The kindly old soul worked there, at the top of her head. Then he asked if I felt ready to begin what I had chosen. He asked if I felt that I had prepared sufficiently, and if I still wanted to take on the body that the girl was ready to surrender. I answered that I was ready, and the others around the bed sent me with their love and encouragement. That is all I remember until I awakened without that dreadful headache."

Laura says that now, as she looks back, she can perceive glimpses of being a discarnate in the dark little apartment, and of studying the body in the shower to learn how to operate it. She occasionally worries that she may be imagining these perceptions, but when, at her suggestion, I asked the Guides about it, they wrote: "The recall is so right! She does indeed remember the times before she entered that body and eventually inherited it. Not so hard to recall, when one uses his inner soul memory."

I prodded them to explain how a Walk-in is selected, and they declared: "If one wants to be a Walk-in, his attributes are considered in much the same manner as are those who wish to incarnate in the usual manner. In *A World Beyond* we discussed the 'heavenly computers,' as we laughingly call them, which automatically work with those who are looking for a suitable vehicle in which to return to flesh. These will be seen as a sort of clearing house which assesses all those qualifications and requirements, and determines the best available spot for those wanting to work off entangling karma and return to Schoolhouse Earth.

"Now, let us explain how a body is sometimes prepared for a Walk-in. If a person has had previous lengthy lives and dreads the debilities of old age, yet feels that he has lessons to learn in human form, he may volunteer to be born in the usual manner, and undergo the training of childhood and youth, but then turn over the adult body to another entity. If that person had previously worked off periods of old age with good humor and repose, and now in the present lifetime wishes to depart, he will be seen as one deserving of a replacement. Another entity of goodly mien, who has a talent for working unselfishly and aiding others, will then be considered as a likely substitute. These souls are matched for similar vibrations and empathy, and if they fit well into the groove, the one wishing to enter an adult body will make his presence felt to the one desiring to return to spirit.

"If they seem compatible, and the one in possession of the body definitely decides to withdraw, then the substitution is made through the help of other discarnates gifted in this type of endeavor. It will be seen that this is not undertaken lightly, and that the transfer of memory pattern to the Walk-in is not without some difficulty, since the one arriving here in spirit also retains his full faculty, the same as if he had died naturally.

"But the akashic records are the source for both, since no single thought or word or deed is lost to that noble document. Even as you do not remember every act or thought of yours since babyhood, so one is not expected to recall everything while in physical body, and the Walk-in will not need a complete record while in flesh. But it is never lost, and it becomes a permanent record of the one who decides to withdraw, while the Walk-in assumes obligation only for his own conduct after the transition of egos has been effected."

I asked the Guides if they could give me a few examples of Walk-ins and Walk-outs, since Laura's substitution is the only one I know about in detail. They responded by writing: "A woman is in the throes of childbirth, and having an extremely difficult delivery. She wishes she had never become pregnant, and is no longer fond of her husband. In such a case, she may decide that she wishes to relinquish her body to another, who has studied it during the months while the owner was fretting about her condition, hating pregnancy, and not wanting a child by that man. This incoming entity may have yearned for children in a previous life and been denied them; so she will step in, undergo the rigors of the birthing, and become the mother who will raise the child and work out a compromise with the father. She may eventually break the marital bond as she goes about her own projects, while never for a moment forgetting the child whose care she has undertaken, or she may learn to love the father. Such a case is not as rare as you may think."

They next cited an instance of a man who feels that he has missed the boat. "He wishes to be a better husband and a more useful citizen, but at every turn he seems stymied in finding the kind of job he feels would contribute to humanity while at the same time providing him with personal satisfaction. Let us say he was educated to be an accountant, but wishes that he were in the law. It is too late to start that new career because of his responsibilities as a husband and father. He resents those responsibilities and will wish so fervently to be rid of the dilemma that he will automatically attract an entity who will try to counsel with him in his dreams and stir him in his waking hours. But if the owner of the body wishes to find peace in the spirit plane, he may surrender the body during sleep. The newcomer may recall the substitution merely as a vivid dream, on awakening, and for a short time feel disoriented until he realizes what has transpired. Sometimes the Walk-in will fall in love with the wife, and serenity will shine forth in the family for the first time in many years."

The Guides said that the initial disorientation lasts only a few hours or days, adding: "As the entity tries out the new body, and the thinking processes of a physical brain which is so much slower in its processes than we are in our means of expression and sensing here, he will gain confidence. He may not for a time remember the transition, or who he was before he entered the body, but he will tap into the memory bank of the person whose body he has entered, and soon will feel confident, aware, awake, and full of energy. Love will pour from him toward those about him, and if he encounters one whom the departing entity had heartily disliked, that person may be amazed at the warmth and friendliness now radiating from him."

CHAPTER VII

Brotherhoods and Group Mind

Among the more intriguing aspects of the New Age is the role that Brotherhoods and Group Minds are said to be playing in preparing mankind for the Aquarian Age and the wave of the future. Through discussions with Laura and Miriam I have learned that there are sixty Serving Brotherhoods, each committed to a particular aspect in the evolution of mankind.

According to ancient, esoteric teachings, there are only four basic commandments for all sentient beings: First, you shall work and serve. Second, you shall learn and grow in wisdom, understanding, and compassion. Third, you shall evolve in terms of your inner being. Fourth, you shall eventually return to the Source from whence you came, as perfected beings.

Through a series of fortuitous events, I was made acquainted with a highly evolved Walk-in who is currently living in the Southwest, and who, recognizing the serious intent of this book, has been extremely helpful in explaining some of my puzzlements about Brotherhoods, and suggesting questions along this line for my Guides.

Michael, as I choose to call him, belongs to the Brotherhood of the Spiral, whose membership is composed of not less than two hundred incarnates at any given time, and approximately six thousand discarnates. This particular group might also be termed the Brotherhood of the Mind, since it is dedicated to opening minds, freeing them from shackles, and bringing awareness to all members of the human race.

Another of the Brotherhoods is pledged to the unfoldment of compassionate justice, with its creed, "Do not do unto another what you would not want him to do to you." Jesus Christ, Confucius, and many other teachers of wisdom have enunciated that golden rule in slightly differing words throughout the ages.

A third Brotherhood is devoted to fair play in all dealings, whether social or business. A fourth is dedicated to bringing in new ideas that will promote a more equitable society, with the ultimate realization that all men are indeed brothers. In fact, every facet of human evolution is dealt with by the sixty Brotherhoods, each concentrating on its own particular segment of the whole. The smallest Brotherhoods are said to have about seven hundred members, and the largest around two hundred thousand, both incarnate and discarnate, with the latter in the preponderance.

Michael told me that many people living today belong to one or another of these Serving Brotherhoods, which operate throughout the world, without realizing that within each one is an Inner (or Closed) Brotherhood with its own individual Group Mind that has been growing and evolving for untold thousands of years. "When an Inner Brotherhood has been in existence long enough, with sufficient members who are strongly enough committed and dedicated to its goals, a Group Mind gradually forms," he said. "This Mind then becomes a consensus of all the knowledge and experience of its members, each of whom can draw on it through mental telepathy."

Because it is a difficult subject to comprehend, Michael gave this further explanation: "Group Mind is something you cannot make happen. It is something that grows from the living mental vibrations and energies of beings who are dedicated to an evolutionary goal or purpose that will give benefit to all sentient beings. Over the ages, as members of these Inner Brotherhoods work and strive and live toward that goal, the Group Mind forms and grows in strength. And the Group Mind can draw on the mind of anyone who's in it, for any information or knowledge or experience, where it's needed elsewhere. But it can only be used in serving and helping others. It cannot be used for selfish purposes, or that member will be denied access to it. Now and then the Group Mind of one Inner Brotherhood will exchange knowledge or experience or information with another Group Mind, through mental telepathy. To restate this in simple terms: Within a Serving Brotherhood, which is something like an outer cloak, there is also an Inner, or Closed, Brotherhood, and it is these Inner Brotherhoods that have developed their own Group Minds during the thousands of years of their existence."

I wanted to know how this mysterious form of telepathy operates between incarnates and discarnates, and he replied: "Group Mind is a fifth-dimension phenomenon. It can manifest in the third and fourth dimensions, and even reach up into the sixth, where your Guides are now. But in the third dimension where all humans are while in flesh, it is only those belonging to the Inner Brotherhoods who are a part of the Group Mind and can readily link into it."

I asked Michael how the rest of us can learn more about the Inner Brotherhoods and perhaps become members. His response—a rather discouraging one for most of us mortals—was this: "The fastest way to find out about such a Brotherhood is to live a highly ethical life, both inwardly and outwardly, treating every other human being as if he were your brother or sister. To do this you have to conquer all dislike of races, groups, and individuals, and you have to live your beliefs for two or three years. If you can do that, someone will come to you and give you certain information. If you can't, he won't. You must demonstrate for at least two years that you can be selfless, not selfish; fair and equitable, not greedy. You must demonstrate a compassion that overcomes human dislikes. If you can't do it, you're not ready. You wouldn't be able to stand the discipline. You have to be willing to do your own work of inner evolution. If you can do it for two years, you'll have six months to think it over before joining a Brotherhood, and then you will begin a seven-year testing period."

Michael asserted, and my Guides verified, that five of the sixty Serving Brotherhoods are composed entirely of Walk-ins, or of entities who in a previous life had been Walk-ins, and that one of their major functions is to assist those who are entering directly into adult bodies. Without the help of one of these five Brotherhoods, it is said to be impossible for a Walk-in to take over human form.

"Experience, after all, is the best teacher," the Guides commented. "The memberships of these five Brotherhoods are comprised of both incarnates and discarnates, especially the latter, since one tends always to remain a member, whether in body or in spirit. But they usually keep a minimum of two hundred members incarnate to assist Walk-ins at the physical level."

Having read so many references to ashrams and communes in recent years, I was curious to learn whether these might actually be a sort of headquarters for Walk-ins and Brotherhoods, but the Guides quickly set me straight. Replying in the negative, they wrote: "As to ashrams and communes, they are accepted nearly everywhere now, although some communities, not yet aware of their vast potential for good in the crisis to come, resent their settlement nearby. There was a lengthy shakedown period in the nineteen fifties and sixties when many of them became unwelcome because of their harboring of youths in revolt, with their employment of free sex and hard drugs. Those problems are gradually fading, and more serious-minded, more stable communities are taking over the management and becoming more selective of the members they admit. These new communes are working hard to erase the bad image of the fifties and sixties, and are earnestly seeking more direct communion with universal energies and the cosmic force. Some Walk-ins are on the periphery of a few of these communal groups, and are counseling them when asked, but Walk-ins do not constitute the membership.

"The Brotherhoods are far older and more esoteric communities, with much higher life-energy levels and a more directed force, where the vows of selfless service and obedience to the Brotherhood are rigidly enforced. The Group Mind of such a Brotherhood grows and evolves into a divine inspiration, becoming a power center where communion is readily established between incarnates and discarnates."

The Guides' use of the term "power center" whetted my curiosity. My Walk-in friends have occasionally spoken of "power points" and "transition centers" such as Stonehenge and Glastonbury in England, but they have seemed rather reticent to discuss the subject. I therefore asked the Guides for elaboration, and they wrote: "There are transition centers on the planet where the vibrations are so high that an ordinary mortal could be seriously affected by the bombardment of sensory particles. These areas are thus screened from interlopers and maintained as meeting places for those of higher advancement, who send and receive signals there both from our plane and the earthly one. They are usually located in wooded and mountainous areas, and streams are also desirable since the flow of pure water has an uplifting effect. The mountainous air is beneficial for higher vibrations, and the trees with their soaring arms help raise the vibratory levels. There are many areas of the globe where these conditions exist: Mount Shasta in northern California, the peaks of Arizona and New Mexico, the green hills of New England, certain areas of the Alps, as well as Central and South American mountain ranges, and, of course, the Himalayas of India and Tibet."

Those who have read *The Teachings of Don Juan* and other books by Carlos Castaneda are familiar with the power centers he describes in Mexico and our western desert area; and Dick Sutphen in *Past Lives, Future Loves* tells of an energy vortex visited by himself and his psychic wife, Trenna, in a mountain valley near Sedona, Arizona.

These power centers, however, have little to do with today's communes, which, according to my friend Michael, have as their long-term purpose the development and evolvement of a more viable life-style as a worthwhile alternative to our deteriorating social scene in which family, church, school, and political establishment are shown to be inadequate to meet today's ethical and moral needs; and it is probable that the self-reliance they are developing will be highly useful as the shift of the axis approaches.

It was Michael who first told me that Walk-ins return from the sixth rather than the fourth dimension, and after I asked the Guides for confirmation, they wrote: "As we told you in *A World Beyond,* there are various dimensions rising up from the incarnate state to the one in which a soul reunites with his Creator. You recall that we were unable to describe that final state, since we here are working in the sixth and into the seventh dimensions. It is true that Walk-ins ordinarily return from the sixth dimension, but not all who frequent this dimension choose to become Walk-ins. That is what we tried to express to you earlier when we said that this is not the dimension to which most souls return at so-called death, but a dimension to which they can aspire if so inclined. The friends whom you call Michael, and Laura, and Miriam are old residents of this sixth dimension; and so, my dear, are you. If you would use a tenth of your powers of remembrance you would know it. Why do you think you were able so quickly to communicate with us, only a few days after first attempting the automatic writing? Because you know this level well, my dear, and you worked with earthlings from here before returning to physical body as an infant.

"There are, as we told you, higher dimensions than this one, just as this is higher than the fourth, fifth, and early stages of the sixth. These are not like stair steps, where you are either on one step or another, you understand, but realms with varying degrees of advancement; just as a student in college will be classed as a junior, but may be making up some sophomore credits and also taking a senior subject."

Michael had called Group Mind "a fifth dimension phenomenon," and the Guides explained: "Man lives in the third dimension while in flesh, and passes into the fourth dimension at physical death, unless he has become so highly evolved spiritually that he will not need to have a resting time there. The fourth dimension gives opportunity for growth, learning, and understanding, and after one has raised his vibratory level to the point where he is ready for new learning, he will wish to progress to a higher dimension. In the fifth dimension where Group Mind radiates, he is learning to project his thoughts, his wisdom, to an almost limitless extent into lower dimensions, as well as upward into the sixth. Incarnates can learn to tune into this flow of wisdom when they realize that they are not bound by the three-dimensional level of earthly existence.

"Some incarnates can and do tap into the sixth dimension from which we function, as you are doing at this moment with the automatic writing. But incarnates do not live in this sixth dimension for any extended period of time unless, like some Eastern adepts, they spend nearly all of their waking hours in contemplative meditation. This is not a wise course for Westerners, who as activists are convinced that work is essential to mankind's progress. You see what we mean? A Westerner ordinarily scorns a person who lives off others, as yogis and lamas do with their begging bowls, while spending their days contemplating God and their navels."

Michael has told me that one of the greatest differences between those of us who are born as babies, and those who return as Walk-ins to adult bodies is that the latter bring in an awareness of the inner meaning and workings of the flow of life. Instead of thinking in terms of one lifetime for each human being, as most of us are taught in childhood, awareness permits one to look down a long series of lives. Awareness is oriented almost to infinity, and is geared to that age-old fourth commandment, "You shall eventually return to the Source from whence you came, as perfected beings."

Mere consciousness is not awareness. Consciousness is of the physical brain, while awareness is of the mind that is a part of the soul, with its soul-memory. Consciousness has to do with thinking and working out problems, while awareness is an inner knowing. It is the higher awareness that tells each human being, "I am." In other words, awareness is the link to the inner being and to the Creator. It is to bring back awareness that Walk-ins are permitted to return to human form as adults.

After musing on these assertions by Michael, I asked the Guides for comments, and they wrote: "Walk-ins indeed return with awareness, and they are able to retain it because, unlike those coming into human form through the birthing process, they do not have it conditioned out of them by parents, teachers, and society. For a time, dazzled by the sudden alteration and the learning process involved in coping with the new body mechanism and leftover tasks, they may not fully exercise this awareness. But if the process is not interrupted by some traumatic event, most Walk-ins will eventually be able to tap into Group Mind, even if they do not actually join a Brotherhood. A Brotherhood imposes discipline which some are unwilling to undertake, but Group Mind is available to all who have awareness, and since Walk-ins automatically return with awareness, they are capable, after a time, of tuning into Group Mind. In fact, all humans have telepathic abilities, which are a part of awareness, if they will only develop and use that ability. It is a part of our God-within-ness.

"Group Mind is a link between incarnates and discarnates, and as one tunes into this network while in the third dimension as an earthling, he is capable of developing to the point where he is in touch with loved ones who have crossed into the fourth dimension. If he is on a sufficiently high plane, he can also tune into the fifth and sixth dimensions."

I was curious to know how Group Mind originated, and the Guides responded: "It has been forming since the beginning of time, just as have the akashic records. It is used both by incarnates and discarnates as they progress and choose their particular fields of endeavor. It grows and expands as each nugget of knowledge is added to it, and as Walk-ins bring in awareness from the sixth dimension, Group Mind continues to be available to them. Awareness is automatic knowledge of the basic elements of life and the laws of the universe. It is an inner knowing, rather than an outer learning, and since Walk-ins generally exercise telepathy, it is simple for them to tune into Group Mind. Just as every thought, word, and deed is recorded in the akashic records, so pertinent awareness is filed within Group Minds."

I had learned from Michael that the five Brotherhoods who work directly with Walk-ins employ something called mind shield to protect the newcomers from discovery while they go about their tasks. Since he did not elaborate, I turned to the Guides for explanation, and they wrote: "Mind shield is a protective cloak to guard one's thoughts from too-wide dissemination. People who are aware of mental telepathy often use it while playing bridge or poker, dropping a mental curtain so that they are not sending forth to their opponents images of the high cards they hold in their hands. In a similar manner, Brotherhoods shield the identity of Walk-ins and other high-minded members from the curious public. There is nothing difficult about it once the principle is understood."

I asked if the number of Brotherhoods would always remain at sixty, and the Guides said there is no magic to the number sixty. "Brotherhoods are in a state of evolution," they continued, "as are all things on the planet and throughout the cosmos. Depending on how you categorize them, there are now sixty, but within them are the Inner groups, and these will expand as time goes by. Nothing is static. All is motion and expansion, including Group Minds. Fifty-eight of the Brotherhoods have Group Minds."

Well, wait a minute! We seemed to have lost two Brotherhoods. But not at all, according to the Guides, who explained: "There are two Brotherhoods without Group Minds, since the members are so highly evolved that the knowledge lies within each of them. These are the avatars, you understand, in whom all knowledge is incarnate for the purposes that the avatar serves. These are perfected beings who have no need to draw on the minds of others." Then, with a gentle dig, they added: "Do not aspire to such as this in the present lifetime. The path is steep, and you have quite a way to go."

Since I have nursed no particular ambition to become an avatar, I took no offense at their put-down, but instead asked why Brotherhoods bother to have outer as well as inner members. "As a means of permitting evolving incarnates to have something to join—a place to develop," they replied, "without initiating them into the inner secrets or esoteric teachings that would be well beyond their present level."

The Guides say that Brotherhoods are going to play "a tremendous part" in the preparation of earthlings for the shift of the axis. "They are so much a part of the universal preparation that they will contribute mightily to the New Age," they continued. "Theirs is a task of enlightenment, and that is what mankind needs at this time. They are already moving to prepare safe havens for those who wish to survive in physical body, and are contacting those both on your side and our side to work in harmony for the common good. We on this side of the open door called death are available to those who would harness the sun's energy as fuel, and we will soon commence to implant in the minds of politicians the means to develop other forms of fuel besides gas, coal, oil, and atomic energy. There are untold dozens of ways to harness the natural energies as yet untapped."

Or as my friend Michael puts it: "There is enough raw kinetic energy locked up in a grain of sand to run all the electrical devices and machinery in Chicago for a year."

He adds that once the human mind learns how to unlock all of the energies in a grain of sand, there will be no further need for fossil fuels.

CHAPTER VIII

Otherwhere

Walk-ins call it the Otherwhere.

That is their colorful term for the particular dimension of life from which they reportedly returned to adult physical bodies to carry out their missions. To my surprise, I have learned that it is not the dimension to which we automatically go when we pass into spirit, but is a highly specialized sphere to which we can earn admission. Intrigued by the references of my new friends to Otherwhere, I asked the Guides for clarification, and they wrote:

"The so-called Otherwhere of which you speak is a part of the sixth dimension where we are now. It is from this sixth dimension that Walk-ins are chosen, because it is the plane in which we are dedicated to working with earthlings to improve humanity. There is no *place* as such, you understand, but a dimension in which we collaborate with each other while working through and with earthlings to achieve the betterment of the human race. The spheres serve various purposes, as we described, but there is no *physical* space, as you know. There are realms and dimensions, and this one to which we are dedicated is a state of being in which we fine-tune to earthlings of similar vibrations. Just as you and Arthur Ford were of similar vibratory level while he was in the flesh, so this level still makes it possible for you to work smoothly together.

"Those here who select this type of endeavor are skilled at aiding ones in physical being who are willing to dedicate a part of their lives to opening up the barriers blocking earthlings from spirit beings. The Walk-ins usually emerge from this realm, for they are interested in helping the masses of people, working through and with them to foster the ideals for which they return to physical being. Thus they work here with us, and when the openings become available [meaning incarnates who wish to walk out of physical being] they volunteer for spots where they feel they can be useful, and where they can compensate for some of their own errors of the past. It is a happy exchange program and one that will be better understood in the years to come."

Since one of my several Walk-in friends said that he deliberately chose to enter a body with certain physical handicaps, I asked the Guides if this is always the case, and they replied: "As to

taking imperfect bodies, there are no other kinds
in human form. The perfect pattern is there [the
etheric body], but always there are imperfections
in flesh incarnate. It is true that some seek out
disabled bodies to repay karmic entanglements of
their own, but many will take whatever is available and make the best of it, for the greater good
of the greater number."

Another day, I further questioned the Guides
about the sixth dimension, asking whether incarnates can learn to tap into its energy field. In a
surprisingly hopeful discourse, they wrote: "We in
this dimension are working regularly with those
who have learned to raise their vibratory levels
to a frequency where we are able to lower ours,
and meld the thoughts. There is energy in abundance here, and those who understand the principle of cosmic energy are able to dip into this pool
at any time and let it flow through them. It is a
healing force and a mental stimulus, and is to be
called upon whenever energies are at a low ebb.
Do not use it as a crutch, but rather as a refueling
station for specific tasks. The Walk-ins who return
to adult bodies are so accustomed to this energy
flow that for a time they are rather overfueled,
since they did not return by the usual routing, as
babies. Those who take over adult bodies are zest-
ful, fired with energy and determination to help
others discover the joys of this renewal process.
They will not lose that zest if they tap into the
reservoirs of strength here, and thus it is better
for them to realize as soon as possible that a substitution of egos has been made in their bodies. In

the years ahead they will be proclaiming this fact to others, and as the process of walking-in is speeded up, there will be less reason to maintain secrecy about their status."

When my friend Laura read this message about the temporary overfueling of Walk-ins, a look of comprehension crossed her pretty face. "Aha! So that's what happened!" Recalling that time a year ago when she apparently took over complete control of her predecessor's body, she said, "While the first morning was awkward and upsetting, this began to be replaced by a tremendous surge of energy and love and beauty. I seemed to begin to realize the overall scope of what the New Age business was all about, and as I met and talked with strangers I found myself surrounding each of them with my love and warmth, and as the love encircled them it brought out a beauty and joy which had earlier been hidden. I seemed to dive into the auras of these new friends that exciting second day, and with one of them I stayed up until the wee hours of the morning, feeling supercharged, as if I had had a good night's sleep and three cups of coffee. I remember that the new friend finally sat back and exclaimed, 'Wow! I can't remember ever being zapped with this much energy before. Where does it all come from?' To say that I was rather overfueled would be an understatement! A few days later, after flying home and returning to my job, I was absolutely loving all of my co-workers, while handling my duties with greater care and skill. I simply thought that the trip had been refreshing. Little did I suspect what might really have happened."

Since I often seem to be tired, it was in a wistful mood that I initiated a morning session by asking the Guides: "Can you tell us ordinary mortals how we can tap into this marvelous energy supply?" Recalling that they had once said, "We're not up there, or out there, we're right here," I further asked if the energy field to which they alluded was here on earth.

No questions seem to faze my unseen friends, who calmly replied: "The life energy is everywhere, untold trillions of units of energy always available to physical beings, as well as to ourselves, who also utilize it in many ways, including help for earthlings. It is in the room where you now write. How else do you contact us, except through cosmic energy? To channel more of it to oneself, one should feel himself floating on a stream of air, wafted aloft by tremendous currents so that one is essentially a part of the Flow. Feel oneself a part of this universal current. If one *becomes* energy, he is obviously energy itself, and has all that he requires. The universe *is* energy. We are all parts of it. It is all one universe. The next dimensions are simply a molecular alteration from the dimension where you are now. We are all parts of the whole, and whether oxygen combined with hydrogen becomes water or is evaporated into air, it is the same element."

Then they offered a fascinating analogy. "To illustrate: You, let us say, are combined just now with other elements to become an earthling, whereas at so-called death you will be freed from these and returned to your pure form. When soul and spirit combine with baser elements they become physical man. When separated from earthly body they again return to their natural element." They added that they would discuss energy in more detail at a later time, in connection with utilization of the Flow.

I mailed a copy of the Guides' message about energy refueling to Laura, and a few days later she wrote to me as follows: "With the Guides' mention of being able to tap into the reservoirs of that energy and strength, I was reminded of the tapping-in that I sometimes do, and I did it again last night. Today I'm on a natural high, loving the whole world and every being in it. I am so glad they mentioned it, because it had temporarily slipped my mind. The process of tapping-in is quite interesting. Usually it happens in the sleep state, but it can also happen while awake. I am still learning about it, but will describe what I perceive at this time.

"It is as if, when I go to sleep, I decide that I need to visit the realm or dimension where I can get a refueling. As anyone, whether a Walk-in or not, can leave his body and travel at will during the sleep state, it is really no problem to go there, and I'm there in a few seconds. I always think of it as a planet in some distant galaxy, but Miriam tells me that it is not a physical place, but a different dimension. In the morning I sometimes recall where I have been or what I have learned while there, but as with dreams the memory tends to fade quickly. Some experiences that I do remember have to do with learning certain basic facts about interaction with other entities—a brief course in human behavior, taught by those most skilled in a particular area. Sometimes if I am dealing with a particular problem, I am helped to understand many factors and options available, and certain energies are channeled into or through my being. But the key word in this experience is love. The beings in that dimension are devoted to service, and when I go there for help or refueling, they completely surround my being with love. When I awaken in the morning I am so filled with love that it radiates out from me and surrounds everyone I know or meet, and I am supercharged with energy."

Returning to the subject of Otherwhere, the Guides said that Betty White was operating from the sixth dimension when, after her physical death, she dictated the material for *The Unobstructed Universe* to her author-husband, Stewart Edward White. They suggested that some quotes from that book might be helpful in explaining the dimension where the Guides are now, but since White's series of psychic books are early classics in the field and still readily obtainable, I will leave it to the readers to pursue that subject if they choose. Personally, I found Betty's mediumistic talents (as reported in *The Betty Book*) fascinating and highly readable while she was still incarnate but esoteric and rather pedantic after she passed into spirit. She did stress, however, that it is all one universe, with those of us in physical body aware only of the obstructed part of it, while discarnates experience the unobstructed whole. There is merely a difference in vibratory levels. For instance, we see the blades of a fan when it is operated at half speed, but look directly through them when it runs at full speed. Similarly, we constantly walk through radio and television beams without awareness of them, just as discarnates move through us and through walls without obstruction.

Inasmuch as Otherwhere is said to be a different dimension from that to which we automatically return when our bodies die, I asked if this was true of Walk-ins too, or if they go directly back to Otherwhere. The Guides replied that Walk-ins, at death, return to the same dimension as others, unless they have so advanced and perfected their souls that they are ready for the highest spheres before reunion with God, but that this holds true for any of us.

"What we are saying here," they continued, "is that Walk-ins are not perfected souls, but ones who are given the right to skip birth and babyhood because of the nature of their projects and the urgency of their tasks. They are high-minded souls rather than exalted ones, if our meaning is clear. They are worthy of entering directly into adult bodies without undergoing birth and schooling there, but on physical death will return to whatever level they have attained on their own path of evolution, just as do all humans. You will remember how different, in *A World Beyond,* were the areas to which various humans passed at death. Some were beside lakes and streams, others in lowly way stations or busy streets. Some were even in marble halls, if they had mentally depicted that as their idea of heaven. Some were far more advanced than others, and quickly settled into temples of learning or into useful tasks, while others frittered away their time.

"For each there is a natural level to which he returns, one where he is comfortable with those of like being, and so it is with Walk-ins. They find their level of attainment with others, as do the rest of us, to assess their past-life errors and accomplishments before selecting a new task or preparing for another go-around in the flesh. We told you of rare exceptions, ones who choose to go almost directly to other adult bodies where available, but this is not the usual pattern. We are simply saying that Otherwhere is the dimension from which Walk-ins return to physical body, having prepared in it here, but it is not the same dimension to which they return at physical death."

But what of Betty White? If the Guides were correct in saying that she had dictated the material for *The Unobstructed Universe* from the sixth dimension, had she not gone there directly upon death? Many years had elapsed since I last read the series of Betty Books, but I have them in my personal library, and after pulling them from the shelf I discovered a fact that previously had made no impression on me. Stewart Edward White had made quite plain that for six months after his wife's death, he had received no communication from her; only an occasional sense of her nearness, such as most of us have experienced following the death of a loved one. Betty White, like Arthur Ford, had apparently made the normal crossover into the fourth dimension before graduating into the sixth, where she could employ her gift for working with earthlings to lift their level of understanding.

My Guides, in patiently seeking to define the difference between the sixth dimension and the plane to which we ordinarily pass at death, further elaborated: "We here in the sixth dimension are functioning in a more electrified, more energized atmosphere than do those souls who return for rest and renewal, to find peace, to visit with loved ones already in spirit, and to prepare quietly for their next incarnation through the natural birth process. When we say electrified it is impossible to make plain, in terms you could understand, the difference between that power which exists as reality in the spirit plane, and the use to which it has been put in physical life. It is a life energy; an intense vibration that permeates every being in whatever form, and extends into the physical plane to a degree that projects the thoughts of discarnates into the minds of incarnates, and vice versa. It is a living stream of energy flow, which extends to every living being in all dimensions."

I was still rather hazy about Otherwhere, assuming it to be identical with the sixth dimension, but the Guides corrected my wrongheadedness, explaining that it is a preparatory level within that sixth dimension for Walk-ins about to return to flesh. "You might think of it as a way station or the road on a map leading from one city to another," they said obligingly. "It is here and also there, if you understand us. There is no *physical* place, but those who wish to become Walk-ins are trained and prepared in Otherwhere by adepts, both discarnates and incarnates, who are members of one of the five Brotherhoods working in this special field. Otherwhere is not really a 'where' at all, but a state of being while undergoing careful, thorough training and discipline for the earthly tasks that lie ahead."

Since the Guides identified Otherwhere as a part of the sixth dimension from which Walk-ins usually return to adult bodies, I began to wonder if my old friend Arthur Ford was thinking of becoming a Walk-in. Readers of my previous books in the psychic field will recall that after I developed the ability to transmit automatic writing, the sessions each day began, "Ruth, this is Lily and the group." Then came the death of Arthur Ford in January 1971, and within a few days he announced his intention of joining the morning sessions in order to bring a clear picture of what occurs when a human being passes into spirit. Thereafter, the daily writing began, "Ruth, this is Lily, Art, and the group."

That is the way it still continues, despite the fact that after his death, while dictating the material for *A World Beyond,* Arthur Ford wrote: "By taking on a short-term project like this one, I will be able to wrap up my earthly duties left undone, make a lasting contribution to the knowledge of all those good folks who looked to me for leader-

ship there in this field, and then go on to other
duties here. I am not going to tie myself down to
years and years of being a message-bearer, as poor
Fletcher [Ford's other-world control while he was
a medium] did for me."

Numerous readers of my subsequent books, noting that the sessions still begin, "Ruth, this is Lily,
Art, and the group," have written to inquire why
Arthur Ford continues to participate. What of his
previous intention to make it only a short-term
project?

Frankly, I wondered too, but it always seemed
rude of me to inquire. Would he think that I was
inhospitable? Heaven knows I welcome the company of Arthur Ford for as long as he is willing
to stick around. It's entirely up to him. But now,
intrigued by the possibility that he might be preparing to return to physical body, I finally mustered the courage to ask these questions: "Does
Arthur plan to become a Walk-in? Does he continue to work through me, and if so, why did he
change his mind about continuing our projects together? Readers often ask." I considered it a nice
touch to put the blame on inquisitive readers,
rather than on my own nosiness.

My unseen friends do not like to be hurried, and
it was therefore several days before they at last
replied to those particular questions, writing:
"Arthur is as much a part of these sessions as ever
he was while dictating the material for A World
Beyond. He decided to remain with this project,
after surveying other fields and recognizing his
superb talent for erasing the barriers between the

living and the so-called dead. He is a fine-tuned
receiver and sender, and from first viewing this
as a short-term project, thus freeing himself for
other realms, he came to realize the urgency of
making these facts available to earthlings, in view
of the short time remaining before the deluge of
souls arrives in this spirit realm at the end of the
century. 'Time enough to become a scholar when
that task is completed,' Arthur says with a smile.
'Right now I am a soldier in the field, doing what
I can to erase the ignorance of human beings, and
prepare them for the shift and the spirit realm
ahead for so many of them.' We in this group whom
you term Guides have no present intention of returning as Walk-ins, feeling that in our present
highly specialized field of endeavor we are best
able, from this vantage point, to serve. There is
no lack of volunteers for Walk-in roles, so we feel
no pressure to return to physical being at present.
And as we have reiterated over and over, we are
all blessed with free will."

Somehow it is deeply reassuring to know that
my old friend Art will continue as a pen pal.

CHAPTER IX

Recognizing Walk-ins

During the writing of this book, my husband, Bob, and I made a trip to England, and on our return the Guides resumed the morning discussions as if there had been no break in their dictation. "Why not commence now," they wrote, "to understand for the readers how they may sense a Walk-in— for there are ways to know him in a crowd—and by protecting him to further his cause? They are ones who have undergone a major adjustment in living and attitude. They are sensitive to the wishes of others, and ready to help in a quiet manner, without effusiveness or desire to attract attention to their helpfulness. Just the opposite of some who loudly proclaim their service to others."

During my absence abroad I had again become assailed with doubts about the reality of Walk-

ins, but the Guides sensed this and moved to re-
assure me, declaring: "Walk-ins are as real as the
girl next door, and we are affirming that they entered those bodies as adults. They are all around
you, and will soon become more apparent as the
world recognizes the need for rapidly stepping up
that process [walking-in] in preparation for the
evil days of the next decade, and the shift of the
axis at the close of the century. They will be declaring themselves publicly before too long, as an
essential step in recognizing the work that will
have to be done rapidly and well."

This seemed rather confusing. The Guides had
emphasized the dire necessity of protecting the
identity of Walk-ins, while also stating that they
will soon be declaring themselves. I therefore
asked for clarification at the next day's session,
and in their imperturbable manner, they wrote:
"The importance of protecting them at the present
time is paramount, for there are not yet enough
of them in physical body to protect each other from
'the slings and arrows of outrageous fortune.' But
they will soon be coming in such large numbers
that there will then be sufficient understanding
of their role to accept them as the sacrificial souls
that they are, working always for the good of others. Until then, if one senses that a friend or acquaintance is a Walk-in he will be wise to keep
it to himself or to speak quietly of his belief to that
person, without spreading it around. We have lessons to learn when in flesh, and one of them is to
protect the privacy of others."

I asked how we might recognize Walk-ins, and

the Guides replied: "There are obvious ways: A distinct alteration of personality and thought patterns. A traumatic experience or severe illness that has altered a person for the better. A willingness to help with others' burdens, and quietly to counsel them without expecting personal reward. An inner poise. A quiet radiance. An unwillingness to exchange harmful gossip about others. A certain reticence about his own hurdles and challenges. Walk-ins are seldom gabby. Their sight is on a rising star, and they do not stoop to maligning others. Take a special look at a member of a city council who speaks wisely when called upon, but seeks no credit for himself. One who is willing for others to take credit for the ideas that he has put into their minds. A calm demeanor. A soul who genuinely likes his fellow beings, without establishing too close ties with any of them."

Tantalized by the last sentence, I asked if Walk-ins form emotional alliances, and the Guides responded: "A Walk-in may fall in love, but only if there are no entangling alliances to be disturbed. They are human while in flesh, after all, but they often seem to be operating at two levels, one in everyday affairs about which they go cheerfully, and the other on a higher plane, as if their thoughts are elsewhere. This does not mean a vagueness, but rather a double operational level, recognizing the needs of workaday life, but sighting goals that seem to be beyond those of their compatriots. Their eyes are tranquil. They are steady.

"If one could read their auras, as some psychics

can, they would note a decided alteration from the body's aura under its previous occupant. They radiate peace, confidence, and human warmth. They are helpful and kind. Sometimes pairs of souls decide to return together. Having formed a strong attachment through many lifetimes, they feel that they will more quickly sense their altered state as Walk-ins by finding each other, and they will thus await an opportunity where perhaps a couple, or two friends, or two siblings have wearied of life and wish to return to spirit. It is always easier to have a friend in the long earth pull, someone who cares and is willing to share one's load."

This latter comment interested me, since Laura and Miriam have apparently tapped into several previous lives, covering a wide range of geographical areas and time sequences, when they were friends or relatives. Laura is a great deal younger than Miriam, and much newer to her present Walk-in role, which was given to her in a different country, so they obviously did not become Walk-ins together; yet Miriam was able to locate and make known to Laura her altered status. She has also helped her to understand the nature of the Walk-in phenomenon, for each new Walk-in is generally contacted by a genuine friend who will help with his adjustment.

Another of my new friends is aware that he took over the body of a soldier who was dying on the battlefield. Since the Guides have stressed that Walk-ins may enter only with the consent of a Walk-out, I asked how an unconscious, dying person could make such an agreement. I was told that when a dying man or woman is unable to support his life energies, which are slipping away from the physical body, the Brotherhoods who work in this field are sometimes able to reanimate it for use by a more energized entity who wishes to enter that badly injured form. "When a baby is born, his umbilical cord must be cut," the Guides explained. "Likewise, when the physical body dies, the so-called silver cord is severed. Because the silver cord belongs to the departing soul, or Walk-out, it must be snapped before a Walk-in enters. That is the reason for the moment or two of unconsciousness that we mentioned earlier. If a body is actually dying, as far as the occupant is concerned, the particular Brotherhoods that are composed of metasurgeons are often able to reanimate that life form for a Walk-in."

Musing about the superior qualities that the Guides have assigned to Walk-ins, and acutely aware of how badly we need heroes in this age of grafting public officials and self-serving leaders, I asked if it would not be better to make their identities known now. "No!" my unseen friends emphatically replied. "We all have a responsibility to protect Walk-ins. Do not tell others if one suspects that a friend or acquaintance is a substitution for the original ego in that body. Wait until that person is ready to reveal himself, for the time will not be far off when they will be accepted as valuable contributors to the community, and honored as such. Their present need is for privacy to prevent witchhunts or crude remarks while they go about the important tasks they chose of their own free will."

Filled with admiration for these high-minded personages, I asked if a Walk-in ever decides to become a Walk-out, because of his own discouragement or severe illness.

"Never!" the Guides promptly responded. "One is under universal discipline when he returns through special privilege as a Walk-in. Having taken the pledge of selflessness, there is now no way that he is permitted to withdraw, short of physical death itself."

Another question was plaguing me. Inasmuch as Walk-ins are said to have such important missions that they are permitted to forego "the time-wasting process of birth and childhood," I wanted to know whether they also regard it as a waste of time to have to complete the projects of those they replace, before getting on with their own tasks.

The Guides replied in the negative, explaining: "No, they do not regard finishing those tasks as time-wasting. It is as much a part of their bargain as it is for the rest of you to secure the right to return to human body as babies. We told you of what we term 'heavenly computers,' which match physical opportunities with the candidates for reentry as babies. It is the same with Walk-ins, except the candidacy there is far more limited, being restricted to those with specific missions to aid mankind, who have schooled for it in what Walk-ins term the Otherwhere. A Walk-in is required to 'tie up the loose ends' of his predecessor in order to be free for the tasks he came in to do. Otherwise, he cannot enter that body."

Because the Guides had earlier identified Mohandas Gandhi as a Walk-in who has not reincarnated, I wondered why, in view of the overwhelming problems in India today, he has not again returned there to an adult body. With remarkable patience for a dull scholar, my unseen tutors replied: "Gandhi succeeded admirably in the task he came in to perform, to demonstrate that a nation can achieve freedom without warfare. He is now working from this side, and reaching far more humans than if he returned to another body, which would not be recognized by others as the habitation for the soul of Gandhi. There is work to be done on this side, so vast in its reaches and so complicated that those with special skills as senders and receivers are urgently needed to prepare earthlings for the shift, while also preparing the spirit dimension for the return of souls in large numbers at the end of this century. Gandhi is serving well."

Here again was an unpleasant reminder of the enormous loss of life, as we think of it, that the Guides foresee when the earth shifts on its axis. To them, of course, it is not loss of life, but graduation from Schoolhouse Earth to a higher dimension of living, and they say of this change: "To prepare for it, so love your neighbor that you feel yourself becoming one with all humanity. This will ease the crossover, as there will seem to be one happy family of souls, delighted to be together while embarking on a new adventure. No one need be lonely or dissatisfied when he has a friend in another human being, so take the time to make friends of all those with whom you come in daily contact: the grocer, the taxi driver, the housewife, the old lady down the street, the child on the corner. All have a place in your own life, and will enrich your life. Take time for other people, feel warmth and love extending out to them and it will return to you in like measure. Give of self and reap the automatic rewards."

I had recently been rereading *Winged Pharaoh* by Joan Grant, with its account of the ancient Egyptian initiation in which one prepared for the priesthood by being entombed alone in a pyramid while leaving the physical body for rather horrifying experiences. Many who entered the initiation experience did not survive it, but those who did emerged with far greater vision and insight. Could this initiation, I wondered, have been a preparation for Walk-ins who could then carry out the duties of the newly initiated priest or priestess?

On putting this question to the Guides, they gave this revealing reply: "The initiation was not so much a project for Walk-ins as it was the purification of spirit by those who entered the underground tombs to commune with their inner selves. They were intent on improving self, so that they would be able to aid others as priests. This was a time of great mental torture, in the sense that we are all members of the human race and unaccustomed to being totally alone for long periods, with nothing to think of except the inner

self. It is a harrowing experience as we begin to
see aspects of ourselves never before noted, and
from which we would escape, as children would
from a bogeyman. There will always be some who
find horrors within, and all of us will have plenty
to delve into that is unpleasant, but the times
when we really look within are as eventful and
rare as a trip to the moon. The initiation provided
that opportunity, and those who survived were the
better for it, purified and stripped of entangling
karma. Thus, if some were there to see only the
good they would find more of it than those who
wish to see evil in others, for they are buoyant
people with a richness of love. There are some
who, in relating their dreams, view them as night-
mares, while others look beyond the outward appearance to the inner quality exposed to view.
Analyzing our dreams is in some respect like the
Egyptian initiation, in that we pull out of our subconscious intimate aspects of ourselves for anal-
ysis. Some of those who went into the Egyptian
initiation chose to withdraw in favor of a substitute, or Walk-in, but that was not the prime purpose of the rite."

Nearly all great religious leaders of past ages
emphasized the importance of finding inner calm
and peace within one's own being. Many of them
were reportedly born of virgins, and were eventually crucified. All of them understood the teaching that there are no miracles, only life energies,
and that what seemed miraculous was simply an
understanding and operation of cosmic law. My
Walk-in friends say that not one of those leaders

called himself a messiah or savior, or came to found a new religion. Jesus Christ claimed no miracles, and told his followers that what he did they would do also, and even greater things. It was the followers who founded religions based on the teachings of those masters.

I therefore submitted to the Guides a partial list of religious leaders which included Krishna, Gautama Siddhartha (the Buddha), Horus, Odin, Zoroaster, Mithra, Thoth, Indra, Tat, Alcides, Bedduru, Quetzalcoatl, Cadmus, Adonis and Quirinus, asking if they were Walk-ins. My Guides replied that most of the ones in the list were avatars rather than Walk-ins, and that they would explain the difference.

"An avatar," they began, "is a superior or perfected soul who returns for a time and then withdraws to the spirit realm, coming and going into physical being at will, but not always wearing the physical body itself. By contrast, those who wish to become Walk-ins have to stay until that life is terminated through normal means, with the body dying. Some of the great spiritual leaders were Walk-ins, and others were avatars. The avatars are able to show themselves to others at a distance, in physical life form, although they may also be seen at the same moment hundreds of miles away. Jesus was seen by his followers and others in human form after his crucifixion, you will recall.

"Quetzalcoatl was a Walk-in, yes, and he was an Atlantean when there were many of them in that island kingdom. And he visited Mexico to reform its agriculture and aid the masses. Krishna and some of the others were avatars at the time that history records them, but had been Walk-ins in previous sojourns in flesh. As to Moses, the Old Testament patriarch, he was a Walk-in from a previous life as an Egyptian hierophant, coming into the adult body of the young Moses, who felt the need to end the captivity of his race."

But what of my new friends' assertion that Walk-ins return not as saviors but as servants, and never take adult bodies in order to found a new religion. If this is true, how could they explain Christ's assertion, "Thou art Peter, and upon this rock I will build my church."

When I put this puzzler to Lily, Art, and the group, they responded: "Yes, the business of 'not saviors but servants' needs a little explanation. All Walk-ins who return to adult bodies are trying to save man from his baser self. Thus they could be termed saviors to that extent, although they are not trying to start a new religion, but to alter man himself through example and gentle hints. Jesus the man was a practicing Jew who had no intention of founding a new church, but when the Christ Spirit entered he saw the desperate need for a widening of the narrow Jewish laws, and felt that Peter would be the one to broaden the base of that movement so that gentiles and all who believed in God might seek the same perfection."

Loving others is said to be the key to spiritual growth, and it was Christ who gave the new commandment, "Love one another."

CHAPTER X

Extraterrestrials

The Byrds of Virginia are among the most illustrious and aristocratic family dynasties in American history. Richard Evelyn Byrd is a direct descendant of William Byrd, the towering colonial leader and planter who built the great house, Westover, on his 179,000-acre James River plantation in the early eighteenth century. Richard's father, Harry Flood Byrd, was the distinguished conservative senator who virtually ran the state of Virginia for forty years, until he retired in 1965 and was succeeded in the U.S. Senate by his eldest son, Harry F. Byrd, Jr., who still holds that seat.

Dick is the namesake nephew of Admiral Richard Evelyn Byrd, the foremost explorer of the early twentieth century, who led flying expeditions over both the North and South poles, and established the first bases in Antarctica before his death in 1957. Dick and his wife, Helen, have occupied Rosemont, his father's beautiful estate near Berryville, Virginia, since the senator's death in 1966, and it is from there that Dick oversees the family's extensive apple orchards and business interests.

I am recounting this bit of family history in order to establish the unimpeachable credibility of the actors in the following drama:

On a warm midsummer evening in 1951, Dick and Helen Byrd tucked their small children into bed and, leaving them in the care of a nursemaid at their estate Avenel, near Berryville, set out for a motion picture theater in Winchester. When the movie ended at 11 P.M., they began the ten-mile drive along Virginia's wooded Route 7 to their home; but at the halfway mark, as they crossed Opequon creek, a break in the woodland permitted them to see a brilliant red glare off to the right, a few miles away. Fearing that their house was on fire, Dick accelerated their speed, and as they continued to watch the night sky, the flaming light shifted so that it appeared to come from their orchards rather than the house.

Rushing along in the car, they surmounted a slight rise in the road, and then beheld a chilling sight. About 1,600 feet ahead, in the center of the intersection where they would turn off Route 7 toward home, a circular object surrounded by what appeared to be a flaming gaseous substance was settling down and landing.

"I slammed hard on the brakes," Dick recalls,

"and edged forward at about five miles per hour. Instantly it began moving toward us, at about our speed."

"We were really frightened," Helen recalls. "We were afraid that whatever it was would engulf us or run over us."

Fortunately the Byrds were abreast of a roadside cafe that was closed for the night, and Dick swung the car into its wide turnaround, so that if necessary they could head rapidly back toward Winchester.

"When we stopped, so did it," Dick said of the object, which he estimated at fifty feet in diameter, including the gaseous flames. "Then I switched off our car lights to see what it would do. We wanted to avoid any maneuver that could bring on hostile action, so we simply sat and watched."

There was no other traffic on the highway in either direction, which seemed unusual to the Byrds, but after a few minutes their curiosity began to overcome their fear. Now convinced that they were staring at a UFO, Dick said, "Maybe they're trying to contact us. I believe I'll drive slowly toward them."

With the car's lights still off, he switched on the ignition and began moving slowly toward the object, but as soon as his intention became apparent the UFO lifted vertically, and took off in a sharp upward climb above the orchards of Rosemont.

"At that, I hit the accelerator hard and we shot down the road and through the gateway to Rosemont," Dick said. "I didn't want to lose sight of it, and Helen and I agreed that the best view of the direction it was taking would be from Dad's verandah."

Senator Byrd was away from home at the time, but Dick and Helen rushed around the house and up the steps to the wide verandah that overlooks the distant Blue Ridge mountains. The spacecraft was still in sight, moving rapidly in a southerly direction, and they watched it for perhaps five minutes until it disappeared into the bright light of the moon, toward which it seemed deliberately to be headed.

Because they were concerned for the safety of their children, the Byrds drove immediately to their own home; but early the next morning they returned to the crossroads near Senator Byrd's estate and minutely searched the area for any sign of singed trees or melted roadway. There was nothing. They thought that since others must also have seen the object, they would surely read about it in the newspapers, but no mention of it appeared.

I asked Helen why they themselves had not reported it to the press, and she replied, "Because of his father's position, Dick was always extremely reticent about taking any action that could possibly reflect on the senator. So many were reporting UFO sightings at that time, that they might have doubted our story."

The next summer, Helen took the children to visit Admiral Byrd at his place on Tunk Lake near Bar Harbor, Maine, and while there she told him of the strange happening.

"The admiral had led such an adventurous life as an explorer and pioneer aviator, and was still so active in aviation and governmental circles that I felt he would be the best one in the family to explain it to me," she said.

Asked for his reaction, she replied, "He was fascinated! He did not doubt my word for a minute, but he seemed so surprised that I felt sure it was not some experimental air force activity. When he telephoned Dick to hear his account of our experience, he chided him for not reporting it immediately, even though he understood Dick's aversion to personal publicity. The admiral himself reported it to the air force, but no explanation has ever been given us for what we saw. It was not phosphorescent gas arising from a marsh, because an intelligence was directing the craft, reacting instantly to whatever maneuvers we made. I have been in heavy mists, fogs, and ice storms. I have seen mirages in the desert, and many other natural phenomena, but this was not a natural phenomenon. There is a psychic instinct within all of us that alerts us to danger from living entities, whether animal or human, and Dick and I felt this, like an electric current passing between us and the operators of the spaceship. It was real. The object within the gaseouslike flame was solid. It had depth, because I could see into it through what resembled portholes."

An account of their adventure has never been published until now, but shortly before Air Force General George S. Brown retired recently as chairman of the Joint Chiefs of Staff, Dick Byrd privately told him about the incident and said he would like to see the air force report on uniden-

tified flying objects. General Brown sent him a
voluminous copy of the report that closed the
books on the government's official investigation
of UFOs. From it he learned that the heaviest
reporting of sightings occurred in 1952, the second
highest in 1951, and that the air force was unable
to provide any explanation whatsoever for twenty
percent of all sightings.

After Dick and Helen Byrd gave me permission
to recount their adventure in this book, I asked
the Guides about it, and they wrote: "The UFO
seen by the Byrds was real, and not of Planet
Earth. We are unable at this late date to say more
about the origins of that particular one, but UFOs
in general are part of the cosmic energy flow, and
are from areas of the galaxy which have learned
to understand and deal with vibrations and energies. As we said earlier [in *The World Before*], they
require assembling in the earth's atmosphere,
after traversing the space from their planetary
home to this planet by means of vibratory energies. It is too complicated for us to explain in terms
that you, at your stage of development as an earthling, could conceivably understand. Suffice it to
say that the UFOs are from outer space, and that
the souls who operate and often inhabit them are
sentient beings who are in a totally different stage
of advancement than are earthlings.

"They will come in increasing numbers as the
time for the earth's shift approaches, for that is
a cosmic event which interests them, just as
earthly beings would line up their top scientists
to observe an expected eclipse of the sun. They

intend no harm, which does not mean that they are not sometimes lethal in their activities when they approach too near to human beings, who to them seem like toys or marionettes. Those extraterrestrial beings who take over the bodies of earthlings are able to operate them without too much difficulty, but they are not many in number."

Afterward, upon reading this last comment, I could scarcely wait until the next day's session to ask if there are actually extraterrestrials walking around here in human flesh.

Replying in the affirmative, the Guides wrote: "Extraterrestrials are indeed on the earth at this time, having come here in what you term UFOs and taken the form of earthlings. They are not as numerous as one might suppose, but they are here, having activated the bodies of some humans who were eager to leave for space journeys to other planets. These are willing exchanges, but it has little to do with Walk-ins, who have always been human beings of earth origin, living and dying and coming again to woman, or to a body that is not wanted by its original owner. Theirs is a mission of uplifting and advancing humanity, whereas the extraterrestrials are primarily here for exploration and a widening understanding between the planets. This will one day perhaps become a more common occurrence, but as of this writing there are only a few of them, and they are rather guarded in their relationship to other beings. They are real enough, but not yet of enough power to influence the conduct of many earthlings."

The following day I pressed for more information, and my unseen friends replied: "The UFOs bring sentient other-world beings in their ships, and a few of these remain to take on various chores of an exploratory nature. They intend no harm to earthlings, but regard their visits as part of a scientific project of great value. Some of them apparently persuaded earthlings to withdraw, or at least to step aside from their bodies for a while and let them operate them. They inhabit them, and sometimes return them to the original occupants who have been anesthetized in certain ways or taken on space voyages without their bodies. As we said, there are too few of them at present to worry about. Were it a long-term project, with conquest intended, there would then be cause for investigation, but they are presently fascinated by the earth's shift that they foresee occurring within the next two decades, and want to study its cause and effect in relation to the universe."

At still another session, the Guides said that UFOs originate from other heavenly bodies that are in similar vibratory plane to Planet Earth. "They come here for inspection and wonderment, and are able, outside the earth's atmosphere, to travel at incredible speeds, so that their journeys are far less laborious than those made from earth to other planets. Rather than being a solid object, they become a life-energy vibration during the journey. They dissolve into component parts and re-form in earth's atmosphere from the pattern of the original. Those who are in contact with these extraterrestrial beings report that they are totally dissimilar to man as he is recognized while in physical body. They are of different dimension and composition, but nevertheless have souls, as do earthlings. Those who have been observed on earth take on the attributes, to some extent, of earthlings, but are able to vanish at will. They are ones who, having attained high skill in their own planets, elected to find ways to enter earth life."

For approximately twenty years after Helen and Richard Byrd narrowly escaped collision with a UFO in Virginia, the newspapers published frequent interviews with people who claimed to have sighted spaceships from other planets. A few even said they had visited them. Because it is difficult for us humans to accept any phenomenon unless we have personally experienced it, many of the claimants were regarded as crackpots. But some were too well known and too widely respected for such a cynical put-down.

On a dark but starlit evening in October 1969, the governor of Georgia and ten other men were standing outside a building in Leary, Georgia, waiting for a meeting of the Lions Club to begin. The time was 7:15 P.M. Looking toward the west, they suddenly beheld a luminous object "about the size of the moon" coming toward them.

"It seemed to move toward us from a distance. It stopped, moved partially away, returned, and then departed," the governor said. "It was bluish at first, then reddish."

That governor, who is now President Jimmy Carter, said that the brilliant object at one point came within approximately three hundred yards of his group, before moving away and eventually disappearing into the distance. Mr. Carter later filed an official statement with the National Investigations Committee of Astral Phenomena (NICAP), a copy of which the White House has made available to me. In it he states that the moon had not yet risen when he and his friends were attracted to the object by its extreme brightness and activity. He said there was no wind, but while they stared in fascination the object, which was sharply outlined against the night sky, changed brightness, shape, and color while performing its maneuvers, and approached quite near to them.

Mr. Carter, a graduate in nuclear physics from the U.S. Naval Academy, placed its location at about thirty degrees above the horizon, and said there was no airport, military, governmental, or research installation in the vicinity of Leary, Georgia. He was so positive that the object was extraterrestrial that during his presidential campaign he was quoted as saying, "If I become President, I'll make every piece of information that this country has about UFO sightings available to the public. I am convinced that UFOs exist, because I have seen one."

Recently we have been hearing less about UFO sightings than during the previous quarter century, and when I asked the Guides for an explanation, they declared: "Because they are finding new ways of entering the earth's atmosphere with less hullabaloo. They want to be around to observe the shift, and for that reason are taking measures to disguise their presence. But the extraterrestrials are coming, in increasing numbers, on purely scientific missions. Most of their entrances into earth's atmosphere are now effected through a quieter means, which permits more of them to remain than if a hefty ship were observed and tracked. The air force is aware of some of this, and is less than open in its reports."

Fascinated anew by the subject, I asked my Walk-in friend Michael what he knew about UFOs, and he said: "Your Guides have correctly stated that extraterrestrials are here for research and study and to try to help all beings. Planet Earth is in quarantine. My information from Group Mind is that earthlings, by once again arriving at atomic technology, are not only polluting Planet Earth, but are unwittingly punching holes in the upper atmosphere and polluting free space. Many of the UFOs are actually around Planet Earth to 'clean up' the pollution in space, so that this prematurely and immoderately released atomic pollution will not harm other planets. The extraterrestrials are indeed fascinated by the coming shift, and want to observe and study events as they occur. Their research project is in terms of millennia, however, not mere centuries or years."

Michael said a few of the Brotherhoods are in contact with extraterrestrials, and when I asked the Guides about this, they replied: "The Brotherhoods are interested in all sentient life forms, but only one or two of them have what you would term direct contact with life forms on other planets. These are the avatar dimensions spoken of earlier, who have no need for Group Mind. The other Brotherhoods are composed of earthlings, both incarnate and discarnate. Thus they have only a limited access to extraterrestrial beings."

My friend Laura told me of a man whom she believes to be an extraterrestrial, and the Guides, upon being asked for comment, wrote: "The one to whom she refers is a spaceman who took the body of an earthling who is now in outer space. He is not a very likeable person, arrogant and superior in his attitude, and he will stay here only until receiving word that his project is completed."

I asked Laura to describe her encounter with the man, and she said, "He is not the most pleasant person to get along with. He seems to regard the others around him as far lower in development and perception. Despite this standoffishness, he has a small group of close friends who seem to accept him for what he is. While others might display in their homes photographs of family members or pleasant scenes, he displays a framed, full-color photograph of a UFO. I was immediately drawn to the picture, and asked him where and when it was taken. All he answered was that the photograph was really an illusion; that it was not a photograph of physical matter, and humans were wrong in perceiving it as physical matter. He would not elaborate, and rudely turned away. Another time I asked him about the coming shift of the earth, and wondered whether it was inevitable. He replied that a rapid shift of the earth's poles would result in devastatingly high winds, such that most above-ground structures would be swept away. He seemed to have thought it out thoroughly, to a level of detail beyond my ability to comprehend. Getting along with this fellow was a real challenge, as he seemed irritated with almost any comment or bit of conversation."

Miriam says the man is an extraterrestrial who, having taken a human body that is beset by chronic illnesses, is terribly unhappy and regrets coming here on the UFO whose picture is framed in his house. "He dislikes having to live among earthlings," she explained, "yet, having chosen to do so and having agreed to complete certain tasks, he is bound by his choice."

This conversation reminded me of a man who sought me out while Bob and I were living in Cuernavaca, Mexico, a few years ago, and who claimed to be from another planet. I was entertained, but unbelieving, since at that time I had not heard of extraterrestrials walking around in human bodies. For that reason, I did not even bother to consult the Guides about him, but I had to admit that for a Mexican he was strange-looking indeed, with red-brown hair and luminous eyes of the same red-brown hue as his hair. He was friendly, highly intelligent, and well mannered. On his second visit he invited me to accompany him by automobile through a nearby mountain pass to a cave near a small Indian settlement, where, he said, I would meet other extraterrestrials and observe their spaceship. Always adventurous, I was eager to go, but my more pragmatic husband flatly refused to permit it, and for once he had his way.

Not knowing quite what to do with my alleged spaceman, I introduced him to my friend Jeanette

Longoria, who was much more interested in UFOs than I was at the time. Jorge (the alleged spaceman) began dropping in at Jeanette's Mexico City house to talk about spaceships, and on each occasion Jeanette's husband, industrialist Octaviano Longoria, and even their houseguests, would mysteriously fall asleep, awakening as soon as he left. Once when the noted couturier Oscar de la Renta was visiting the Longorias he was suffering extreme back pains, but after Jorge held his hands over him Oscar reported that the pain instantly disappeared and did not return throughout his tour.

Just as I was wishing that I knew what had become of Jorge, Jeanette telephoned me in Washington for the first time in nearly a year. She said that after losing all track of Jorge for two years, he had suddenly turned up again in Mexico City to tell her about a spaceship which he claims is buried beneath a pyramid on the outskirts of Mexico City. He said it is one of the ancient ones, and that outer-space vehicles have been visiting Planet Earth for untold centuries.

Jeanette reported that although Jorge still converses in such highly technical scientific terms that he seems to be in another dimension, she was surprised at one outward change in his appearance. His scalp has now developed a bony protuberance in the form of a large horseshoe, which, she says, is clearly visible through his red-brown hair. Jorge insisted that she feel the protuberance, but gave no explanation for its appearance.

I still get a little annoyed with my husband

when I think that he may have caused me to miss a space ride, particularly since the Guides, while commenting on Laura's spaceman, said of Jorge: "The extraterrestrial you met and talked with in Mexico is of a higher type who genuinely likes human beings and wants to learn all that he can about them. He's like a missionary who sincerely wishes to help others."

I do not pretend to be an expert on UFOs, or on any other aspect of the psychic world beyond our three-dimensional earth. I can only pass along to readers, hopefully more advanced than myself, the information that my Guides seem to consider important to mankind's upward spiral. To the limit of my own understanding, it would seem that the Guides have identified three different types of beings who have achieved sufficient advancement to enter our earth plane, and appear in solid form to us, without submitting to the normal process of birth and babyhood.

Apparently the highest achievers in this category are the avatars, who can come and go at will, and who, according to the Guides, are in touch with outer-space beings as well as with humans on Planet Earth. The second type is the Walk-ins, who have always been earthlings but are high-minded, advanced souls who return to adult bodies in order to accelerate the progress of their fellow-men. The third class is the extraterrestrials, who, still few in number, have allegedly found the means of penetrating the earth's atmosphere and occupying the bodies of adult humans, for limited scientific experiments and observations of our planetary changes.

I cannot prove a word of it. I can only pass along what my ordinarily reliable Guides have had to say about it, in the hope that others, more scientifically minded than I am, will make their own contributions to the mystery of eternal life.

CHAPTER XI

The Flow

From time to time my new friends (the Walk-ins) and my unseen friends (the Guides) have made references to "the Flow." The term was new to me, and because they seemed to consider it of paramount importance, I was eager to learn more about it. The Flow, they say, is all around us, in a constantly evolving upward spiral, but the trick is in learning how to let oneself flow with those energies in their currents.

This chapter, then, is an attempt to explain what the Flow is, how we can sense it, become a part of it, utilize its energies to avoid dangers and missteps, and speed our evolution.

The Guides, declaring that all of us are constantly bathed in a sea of energies, initiated their discussion of the Flow in this way: "The entire cosmos is energy. It's not just composed of energy, it *is* energy, and since we are infinitesimal parts of the cosmos, we too are energy. Therefore, when you say that you are tired, you are simply saying that you are out of tune with the universal energy, the cosmic Flow. Get into it, and swim. Submerge yourself in it. Feel yourself as a pulsating, living part of the universe. To swim into the Flow, lie on the floor or on the bed and feel as if you are being swept off headfirst, still in a prone position, and floating into a sea of energy. It's not difficult for one who uses a tenth of his native imagination. Go with the tide. Don't buck it. Energize yourself, and you will begin to awaken that awareness that is too often bred out of human beings from birth onward, with the regimen of feeding, schooling, and mind control imposed by well-meaning parents and teachers. That's why mistakes keep being repeated over and over, and why man's upward progress seems so inert. Those fine people who correct the utterances of children slow their imagination and teach them the same fallacies which they themselves have been spoon-fed throughout their lives. Any baby would know that life is indestructible and that the soul is in a continuing process of birth into body and birth into spirit, ad infinitum. It's the adults who tell him otherwise."

Since Walk-ins, by skipping childhood, are able to avoid this conditioning, they bring in awareness intact, and are thus more easily able to keep themselves within the Flow. I like the way Michael states it: "Awareness often whispers through one's consciousness as intuition or hunches. Once one

mentally lifts himself into the dimension of awareness and lets his inner-life essence remain within
the Flow, his awareness is tuned in, and he can
function far more effectively in his daily life and
activities."

I asked him to explain the difference between
awareness and Flow, and he replied: "Flow is of
all living energies; awareness is of all mind—the
Universal Mind. One of the primary purposes of
Walk-ins is to bring in an awareness of greater
dimensions and greater freedom, and awareness
is in part a sensitivity to the Flow. Many Walk-
ins are not consciously aware of what they are,
yet the awareness of Flow is in them, and they
intuitively know how to remain in the Flow while
attributing their choices to 'hunches.' Intuition is
from awareness, percolating down through human
consciousness. Intuition is a knowing, without
having to reason it."

Because Laura has so recently become a Walk-
in, I queried her about how she learned to get
into the Flow. "I began to pay more careful attention to my intuition," she replied. "I began each
day to see what my overall goals were in this lifetime, and what the overall goals of humanity
might be, and I started listening very carefully
within. It's a matter of quietly choosing, contin-
uously, the direction that seems to be the most
harmonious with one's inner being. Intuition is
one of the facets of awareness. He who gets up in
the morning determined to clear his desk and get
a lot of things done without regard for what may
feel right is bucking the tide and placing himself

out of the Flow. But he who acts from an inner sense of what will work *today* has placed himself in the Flow.

"When I wrote to you in June," Laura continued, "I was in the Flow, for some inner sense told me that this was the time to dangle the idea of Walkins in front of you. I had thought about it earlier, but it never seemed like the right time to contact you. But when the timing felt right, the letter wrote itself. It was done in the Flow, for it reached you at a time when you were most receptive to it. On another day you might have answered it politely and then discarded the letter. Thus it is with the Flow. He who trusts his intuition and places himself in the Flow will seem to ride on a current of energy, and along the way several other factors will fall in line, as if intended."

The Guides describe the Flow as an upward spiral that encircles the entire cosmos, touching on all things and all beings, "but the Flow, as it affects earthlings, is such a gradual encirclement of the planet that the spiraling is barely perceptible. This Flow is available to all, whether aware of it or not," they explained. "It is evolving, growing, altering, and yet never-changing in its patterns. All things are reflected in it—all thoughts and moods and humors. The knowledge is there, and it was this Flow that Bill Gray called the Ring, when he would tell you that he was 'taking my answers off the Ring,' remember?"

(William Gray, who has now passed on, was the remarkable healer whom I called Mr. A, to protect his privacy, in *Born to Heal.*)

Continuing their discussion, the Guides wrote: "One's intuitive forces determine one's own flow within the Flow. If you sense that it is right for you to take a certain action, you are moving in the Flow, and that movement is ever upward. If you are bucking it, you are disturbed, distressed, restless, and unhappy. To move with the Flow is to be in the natural groove. Stay with it, and all is smooth sailing for your projects, your friendships and decisions. Step out of it, and you are floundering. Intuition is the test, for if you know within yourself that something is right, that the time is right, you are rising with the spiraling Flow, and as the Irish say, 'You'll have the wind at your back.' But if you try to pretend to yourself that what you are doing will pass muster, and you go against your conscience; if you try to move when the time does not feel right, then you are stepping out of the Flow, and nothing seems to go right for long."

Shamelessly fishing for a compliment, I asked the Guides, "Am I in the Flow when I am writing this book?" I was hoping, of course, for a resounding yes, but that is not the way my unseen friends respond to my fishing expeditions.

"When you feel that a chapter is right, then you are in the Flow," they responded gravely. "When something bothers you about it, and you feel that it is out of your depth, put it aside for a time, until it suddenly seems to flow into the rest of the material. Don't force anything. Don't accept all without feeling within yourself that it adds to the value of the book. Don't push yourself or your faithful readers out of their depth by taking new ideas whose time for you has not yet come. Stay in the Flow, my dear. You are aware when it's right for you, and through you for your readers."

It was with a sigh of relief, after reading this, that I abandoned a highly technical segment of this chapter having to do with kinetic energies versus life energies in their relation to the Flow. The information had come from my friend Michael, and because I know him to be brilliant and high-minded, I had been struggling for many days with the material, trying to put it into words that I felt would have meaning for my readers and myself, but feeling that it had no real significance in helping to understand the Flow. How marvelous to discover that I had been bucking the Flow, and that if I cast the material aside, I could return to inner harmony. Perhaps I will be ready for such abstruse subjects in my next incarnation.

Laura, who seems more down to earth than Michael, offered several practical analogies of how one can learn to sense the Flow. Anyone who has put his canoe into white water in the spring, she says, knows that the best way to get downstream is to be alert, keep one's direction steady, and ride the smooth water as it rushes around or over rocks. "If you simply plunge forward willy-nilly or try to force against the current you risk nosing under, turning broadside, sinking your canoe, or getting badly injured," she declared. "Likewise, if you place yourself in the Flow, you can ride the currents of energy and reach your goal more quickly, safely, and easily than if you tried to 'make' something happen. But you must learn to sense the Flow. Boys in a white-water canoe learn to sense water currents, having taken their share of spills when they guessed incorrectly. Likewise, glider pilots learn through trial and error to ride the air currents, correctly sensing the likely updrafts. The pilots of hot-air balloons learn to read the signs given by cloud shapes, and sense which altitudes have currents that will take them in the direction they want to go. Jet pilots make better time when they fly with tail winds or choose altitudes where turbulence is lower. If you would be in the Flow, riding its currents of energy, you must learn to sense the direction of flow for any given project on any given day."

I asked how this could be accomplished, and she replied: "First, look toward your immediate goal and know that you will reach it. When it is time to choose between one direction or another, simply pause for a moment, blank your mind, and listen to your intuition. Don't try to reason with logic. Your own inner sense will tell you which choice to make. If it is any more meaningful, ask for guidance from whatever source is most comfortable for you, whether divine inspiration, prayer, or help from discarnates. Try being in the Flow as often as you think of it. As you test for yourself, you will find that it works. Decisions come more easily and goals are more readily reached. When you place yourself in the direction that feels the most harmonious, then you will be carried along to the accomplishment of each succeeding goal with greater ease."

Being in the Flow can help you to escape from danger. Newspapers often carry stories about people who, at the last minute, decided not to take a particular plane or train that subsequently crashed. "Something told me not to take it," they are quoted as saying, "even though I held a ticket on it." They were in the Flow, whether or not they realized it, and listening to their intuition.

Laura says of these phenomena, "I remember reading of studies done on train accidents, where on the day of a serious mishap fewer passengers than usual were on the problem train. I recall the plane that crashed across a busy highway at rush hour in New York, and, as if by a miracle, there happened to be no cars on the highway at the point of impact. If you remain in the Flow and trust your inner guidance, you will find that in an accident or a disaster your intuition will guide you to reach safety, and to help others to safety. For one who remains in the Flow, disasters are merely learning experiences, challenges to work through, stepping stones along an upward path."

A strongly visualized goal becomes a spiritual magnet to which the necessary tools are drawn if one remains in the Flow. To illustrate, one of my Walk-in friends who does not have much money seems instinctively to know when to leave his house in order to hitch a safe and comfortable ride to his destination. He has had no scary encounters, and he has never had to wait for more than a few minutes for a car to pick him up. More than once, when driving to work, Laura has suddenly left home a half hour early, or varied her normal route, for no apparent reason other than that an inner prompting told her to do so. Later she has learned of a disastrous pile-up of cars at the place on the highway where she would otherwise have been at that exact time.

Just as animals living in the wild state sense danger and flee, so most of us are born with this intuitive sense, but it is often disciplined out of us in our youth. The Walk-in enters without this childhood conditioning, and despite the memory patterns inherited from the previous owner of his body, he soon begins to see that the old way of thinking does not work nearly as well as what he perceives as "a new outlook." He may not yet know that he is a Walk-in, but having brought in awareness he will instinctively trust his intuition every day. He will set goals, and by his intuitive trust or inner knowing will accomplish his purpose, because opportunities will open and the right situations or tools will seem to fall into his path at just the right moment. Others, marveling at his success in an endeavor that they had considered impossible, will say that he had "lucky breaks," when what he actually did was to place himself in the Flow, and move along with the current.

Enchanted by the seemingly magical powers of the Flow, I asked the Guides if there was a technique that I could use in putting the business problems of a certain friend into the Flow, so that they could more easily be solved for him.

"The answer is no," they replied. "Each will have to do that for himself, but the Flow is there for anyone to meld into, if he so desires. There is no way for another to put you into the Flow. We are here to help point the way, but each person must himself flow into it. Not everyone is interested in becoming a part of the Flow. It sometimes entails going against one's financial aspirations, for if one is hell-bent on getting money he will perhaps be stepping on others' toes, or even going against his own conscience. The Flow works for unselfish purposes, but is not a cure-all for getting or making money. Let that be made clear! This is not one of those do-it-yourself articles on how to make a million or swing a big deal or break the bank at Monte Carlo. The Flow is an evolutionary spiral for the uplifting of the entire human race and all that touches it. Therefore, the way to find inner peace, tranquility, accomplishment, and love is to put oneself into the Flow through harmonious thoughts and helpfulness to others. It will move one toward his goals, if they are worthy. It will also protect those who utilize it from danger, for the sensing of the Flow guides one to safe areas and to safe time sequences."

I asked the Guides if they could be more specific about how to get into the Flow, and they responded: "When the inner voice of conscience tells us right from wrong, and we follow that instinct, we are in the Flow. When our intuition says 'not now,' or 'now is the time to make that important telephone call,' we are in the Flow. The Flow is simply the stream of life energy that is spiraling aloft and will take us with it, if we heed the inner wisdom. When you thwart that spiraling flow you are bucking head winds, and will have to stumble or fall back. Really a simple, basic law of the universe! As the Bible says, "To everything there is a season, and a time to every purpose under the heaven.' By heeding the inner voice, one realizes when it is right for him. Why force oneself to rush out into a stormy night and hurl oneself against driving rain, when in another hour or so the night will be calm and starry? Life is like that. Choose carefully the right time to go for the important interview or to submit an article for publication. Feel it within yourself, that this is *your* time to move, or just to wait quietly until the wisdom within says go."

Inasmuch as both the Guides and my Walk-in friends have stressed that there is a "time" to take action, and a "time" to wait until an inner voice tells us to act, I asked Michael if this philosophy might not lead to endless procrastination. What happens if a person continually says he doesn't feel like doing anything that day but sleeping or watching television or goofing off?

"He's copping out," Michael replied. "To be in the Flow means that you accept the responsibility for your own evolution. Constantly to sleep or to kill time is a cop-out. You have to make a contribution, because the first commandment of life is 'You shall work and serve.' That doesn't mean you're going to serve yourself. It means you're going to serve life. And until you've worked and served life, you are not ready for the second commandment, to 'Learn and grow.' You are not evolving. When one chooses to be in the Flow, he chooses to listen to the direction that seems the most harmonious. He listens to his intuition. He works and serves."

But all of us have free will. So what if a person couldn't care less about being in the Flow, and "serving life"?

"A lot of people are like that. They choose the material and go after wealth, not realizing that it is illusion," Michael answered. "They amass lots of wealth, but when they eventually pass into the spirit stage the wealth doesn't go with them, so what have they gained in evolution? They may go through sixty lifetimes like that, before they're ready to start looking for the truth, for the reality. Each entity has freedom to choose how rapidly he will evolve. We can go to all the sandlot baseball games we want to along the way, but sooner or later we're going to get tired of sandlot baseball, and look for something that has greater depth and more lasting meaning."

"So all of us will eventually evolve to the point where we are in the Flow?" I asked.

"Yes," he replied. "Right on!"

One morning the Guides proposed another exercise which they said could help us get into the Flow. Declaring that there are various ways to become "a living stream of energy," they counseled: "When one is in bed, he can sense the force of the Flow more easily if he lies with his head to the north, so that he is in line with the polar energies. Then, as he feels himself becoming a part of the earth's rhythm he will mentally float off into the stratosphere, with the earth becoming smaller and smaller as it recedes from his inner view. As he gently moves along in outer space the earth's circumference has long since been left behind, and in a spiral motion he is as completely immersed in cosmic rhythms as if he were a star in fixed motion, orbiting around other bodies and feeling himself a part of the divinity. There is something special in this feeling of oneness with the cosmic force. Then, as one eventually descends to his bed, he realizes the awesome majesty of the firmament, and the miniscule part that he is playing, so that problems which have been disturbing him seem as child's play to solve. How easy, after such a mental adventure, to see that what seemed insurmountable is solving itself, for when one chooses between two courses of action, there is always one which seems right, whereas the other has too many ands, ifs, and buts about it. Take that course which feels right, as if it too were a part of the cosmic force, and there will be no nagging doubts. The 'still, small voice within' is always right, and when one taps into the cosmic sweep of events, one sees how right that particular voice has been."

The Guides say that it is easy for us to feel ourselves a part of this stream of universal life energies, if we will only begin to practice it. "You ride in the orbit, gently feeling yourself a part of this great current that encircles the earth, as it does all planets which sustain life forms," they averred. "A dead planet such as the moon is one whose energy flow has dissolved and gone back into the stratosphere. This Flow is a part of life, and energizes all life. It is there, whether you sense it or not, but in order to use it to individual advantage, one should feed himself into that stream for a time, feeling himself a part of the energy flow, and reenergizing himself in the process. If one would do this several times daily during periods of stress or exhaustion, he would find himself literally walking on air. It is a vital force, and is a part of the universal laws of life."

My friend Laura urges that all of us begin to practice "being in the Flow" whenever we think of it, and listen to our intuition. Getting the hang of it now, she says, can save the lives of those who want to survive the shift of the axis in physical body. Understanding of the Flow can help whole groups of survivors to reach areas of safety in plenty of time, provide them with sufficient food and shelter, and aid them with the monumental task of rebuilding a better world. We will hear more about that in a subsequent chapter.

CHAPTER XII

Channeling the Energies

Would you like to be able to conjure up empty parking spaces on crowded streets? Dissolve clouds? Heal your friends? Enjoy bountiful good health? Produce prize-winning flowers and vegetables of singular perfection?

Then learn to use the energies!

The Guides say that we are all swimming in an inexhaustible sea of energies, and that those who seemingly perform miracles simply know how to utilize the energies. It's apparently as simple as the law of gravity, if we understand the principle.

By testing some of these basic truths now, and proving their workability, we will be better equipped to withstand the rigors of the two decades remaining in this century. These tried-and-true methods may be our best "survival kit."

Let's begin by dissolving a cloud. Thousands of people have accomplished this, simply by believing that it can be done. Professor Charles H. Hapgood, author of several scientific books, for one of which Albert Einstein wrote the introduction, amazed a group of his friends by successfully performing this feat three times in succession.

To test it for yourself, select a small cloud and give it your undivided concentration for several minutes. Mentally tell it to dissolve, and picture energies flowing through you and up to the cloud to increase its temperature. Keep watching, and it will disappear as if by magic.

My friend Laura has proved it to her own satisfaction. Having heard of the phenomenon, she was eager to test it, and says of that experience: "I was in the backyard hanging up laundry. It was one of those days when fluffy clouds were passing overhead against a deep blue sky, a perfect day for experimenting. Much to my surprise, the first cloud I tried disappeared completely within four minutes. That could have been coincidence, but I tried a second and then a third and in each instance the cloud thinned, faded, and then vanished. At that point I was forced to think very seriously about the power of thought. In willing a small cloud to disappear, I had a graphic demonstration that human thought can effect changes in physical matter, even if the object is miles away. This was no longer theory. I had tried it out and proved it to myself. I began to realize that if one human being can control a cloud by using only the mind, enormous good could be accomplished sim-

ply by the power of thought, if we all worked together."

The Guides say that even World War III, which
looms darkly on the horizon, can be prevented if
we all begin now to concentrate our thoughts on
a peaceful world. The energies will work toward
that goal.

Miriam, who is more advanced than most of us,
asks with a dry chuckle: "Why bother to dissolve
clouds? Why not concentrate on forming clouds,
or shaping them? It's much more artistic."

Another beginner's experiment to prove the
power of the mind is producing an empty parking
space where none exists. This is the basic Law of
Manifestation. Strongly visualize what you need,
then follow your own intuition, stay in the Flow,
and you will be led to it. To manifest a parking
space, choose a time when there is an imperative
need for one. If you have circled the block without
success, concentrate on the area nearest your destination, and know that a parking space will materialize for you there. Send forth the energies,
and as you near the coveted place, a car will pull
out of it at the right time.

Rhoda Montgomery, my late sister-in-law, who
first introduced me to psychic phenomena, used
to drive her aged mother to the doctor's office in
a downtown area that was always jammed with
automobiles. Since her mother was too frail for
much walking, Rhoda would mentally say to her
deceased father, "All right, Papa, if you want me
to take Mama to the doctor, find me a parking
place in front of the building." Invariably a parked

car would pull out just as she reached the desired space. This would seem to demonstrate the point that Laura made in speaking of the Flow. If it seems more natural to request a needed object through prayer, or divine intercession, or help from discarnates, do so. The energies are being set in motion through your own concentration on the need.

Laura regularly manifests parking spaces. I have tried it on occasion, when the need was urgent, and have found that it works. I know of a hard-pressed mother who visualized a warm coat for her little girl, only to have a neighbor ask if she could pass on to her some winter clothing that her own child had outgrown. Another woman desperately needed a gas range, and after visualizing it for a couple of days, an acquaintance mentioned that she would like to get rid of one that she was replacing with electricity. Findhorn, the famous community in northern Scotland, is a good example of the workings of this law, since its greenhouse, its bungalows, and numberless other needed objects were "manifested" by its founder, Peter Caddy.

"Or if you want a closer-to-home example of the Law of Manifestation," Laura said, with a pixie grin, "look at us! I used to visualize meeting my favorite writer, Ruth Montgomery. And I would picture myself being able to encourage her and help her to continue writing. It really works, you see?"

It was rather a strange sensation, to realize that energies projected toward me from a stranger had actually prompted me to write this book. Yet I had to admit that of the tens of thousands of letters I have received from my unknown readers, this was the first instance in which I had been so captivated that I had actually gone to see the letter writer.

Laura, in discussing this chapter, emphasized, "It is important to give to life, for life will give to you as you yourself give. One cannot simply keep manifesting material needs for selfish reasons, because if the reasons are selfish the law will cease to work."

Findhorn, about which the public television network recently ran an hour-long documentary, is an excellent demonstration of another way to put the energies to work for a good cause. Nearly everyone by now has heard of that phenomenal community, established in 1962 on a barren stretch of gorse and sand where the agricultural experts said that nothing but the most tenacious weeds would grow, which has blossomed into a veritable Garden of Eden. Through visualizing their needs, including a greenhouse, and projecting the energies and love to every stone and seed and human task, while scorning chemical fertilizers and noxious sprays, the Caddys and their friends were soon harvesting incredible crops, including some cabbages weighing approximately forty pounds each. These are the kinds of experiments and the types of communal groups that the Guides say will be of inestimable benefit in helping others to cope with the shift of the axis at the close of the century.

If the power of thought on energies can dissolve

clouds, manifest parking spaces or greenhouses, and produce record-breaking crops, it can obviously affect bodies as well. If you like, test out the healing energies first on a household pet. Last year, a veterinarian told my cousin that nothing could be done for his aging dog, who was so stiff from arthritis that she could scarcely walk. After studying the X-rays, which clearly delineated calcium deposits in the joints, my cousin decided to try a healing technique that he had read about in a magazine. Each evening for about ten minutes he would take the dog on his lap, pet her, and then picture warmth and energy flowing through his arms and hands into the calcium deposits. Simultaneously, he visualized the deposits breaking down and being absorbed into the bloodstream, so that they could pass out of the body as waste. He reports that while channeling the energies, he could feel a tingling and warmth in his hands and arms, and after a week of this treatment the pet became so lively that she began jumping up on chairs. At first he thought that the recovery might have been coincidental, but when the stiffness began to return he went back to channeling the energies into her joints, and the dog has had no recurrence of the problem that the vet had pronounced incurable.

Edgar Cayce cautioned his followers not to place people on their prayer-healing lists unless they themselves requested it. When I asked the Guides to explain the principle involved, they wrote: "It is important that the person wants to be healed, for unless he does, interfering relatives and friends can prolong a term in Schoolhouse Earth which is completed. Those who wish to be healed, and feel that there is a purpose yet to be served in physical being, should alert those around him to that desire, and they in unison should visualize the person as completely whole, lithely swinging down the street or going about important tasks with a smile on his lips. Do not, for selfish reasons, try to stay the passing of another. Always remember the purpose to be served, while realizing that the best life is in spirit, so why prolong the stay of one whose work is about finished? As to healing from a less-than-fatal ailment, it is good to wish that the pain or discomfort leave that body. There is strength in numbers, and if a group gathers together the energies are drawn more rapidly. They need not cluster around the patient's bed. The energies are directed to that person whether or not he is physically present. It is important not to tell the energies what to do. Let the energies go to work. They know much better than you do what is needed."

Miriam uses a system that is said to be safer than picturing tissue, cells, or masses. She mentally places the patient within a golden ovoid that is flecked with light green—which psychics call the healing color—blesses him, and then lets the energies go to work.

Many others, of course, effectively use the power of prayer, and when I asked the Guides to explain what happens with prayer, and with blessings, they wrote: "The power of prayer transcends all other energy for mankind. This is direct approach

to the Creative Force, and melds with the universal power of love. Prayer goes to the source of all
energy and all power. If one unselfishly asks of
God, that wish is a part of the creative whole. To
request blessings for others is a part of the force
of love. To ask that rivals or enemies be blessed
is a breaking-down of barriers which separate one
from another. To ask that others be blessed is to
recapture the oneness of all egos, the oneship with
God, the wholeness of the Creative Force. As to
healing by turning over the problem to the energies, why not? They are a creative force in action."

Miriam has encouraged Laura to bless each
piece of work as it comes into her hands, and to
send it on with a blessing when she has completed
it. This, of course, is a mental process, not a moving of one's hand over an object, as a priest often
does. Laura says of it: "When I wish to bless someone, I let flow a stream of energies from somewhere beyond me, out to and around and through
the person blessed. It happens in the twinkling of
an eye, with no words. It is rather like surrounding
them with love. I now do the same with my work."

A great deal has been written in recent years
about the power of prayer on plants. Scientist
Cleve Backster, biologist Jagadis Chandra Bose,
the Reverend Franklin Loehr, Professor Hapgood,
and others have conducted controlled scientific
experiments in this field, all seemingly proving
that plants thrive on love or prayer, but may
wither and die if hate is directed their way. Just
as our thoughts can affect people, pets, clouds, and
inanimate objects, so do they affect living plants.

This discovery takes on added importance if we believe the dire events the Guides foresee for the remainder of this century. An ability to grow large amounts of food in unfertilized areas of the world will mean the difference between life and death for those who survive the famine of the 1980s and the later shift of the axis, when so much of our cultivated land disappears beneath the seas, while new lands emerge. When a plant is loved and appreciated and when we visualize it as healthy and productive, it will thrive. Curse it or spend your time feeling sorry for yourself, and it tends to sicken and die. Plants respond to our vibrations. They also have reactions of their own. Backster, by attaching the electrodes of a polygraph (lie-detecting device) to his houseplants, discovered that they reacted violently when live shrimp were dropped into boiling water. They registered apprehension at the approach of a dog, and trembled when voices were raised in anger. When plants and fruit trees become critical to our own survival, we would do well to remember that a loved plant finds its easier to be healthy than one that is ignored or taken for granted.

By the same token, we can improve our own state of being by visualizing ourselves as healthy and at peace with others. If we want to enjoy vibrant good health, we can manifest it for ourselves by thinking in those terms. If you visualize yourself as ill, or fear that a situation will develop that can prevent you from being active, you may subconsciously begin making the decisions which can lead to that situation. But when we picture our body as working in health and inner harmony, we improve our attitude and attract the healing energies that are all about us. Some feel that cancer is the result of unhealthy or unhappy attitudes toward life.

I asked the Guides about this, and they replied: "Not all persons are unhealthy through a subconscious wish to be so. Some are repaying karmic debts, and others are weak in certain areas through birth defect or childhood exposures and mishaps. Some are ailing for valid reasons, but there are so many psychosomatic causes of illness as to defy description. Think healthy! Be healthy!"

Because of the emphasis placed on the power of thought, I urged the Guides to explain in greater detail how the energies can work for us.

"The energies are there to be used," they wrote, "and if proper respect is paid to them, they will perform countless tasks that otherwise would be impossible. Let us take, for example, a man who wishes to have a different job in order to provide better for his family. He will visualize the work that he wishes to be doing and the salary that he requires in order to meet adequately his living costs; then he will send out the energies by believing that it will happen, and seeing himself in that job, happy and valuable as a contributor to the work force. If the goal is reasonable, and if he is adequately trained and fitted for the position, he will be amazed to discover how quickly that dream is realized. Remember that it must be a position for which he is qualified, and one within his potentials. He will, of course, have to put forth his own efforts to secure it, but by concentrating on that one line of work, in one particular company, he will start the energies that will affect the decision of those who do the hiring, and the job will be his.

"As to clouds, the energies are indeed capable of warming and puffing away a fleecy cloud. That does not mean that one man is able to will a leaden sky to become blue, for collective energies are needed there, as with the Indian rain dances of yore. But the energies will work for individuals in their own affairs if the motive is unselfish."

Just as any of us can work with healing energies, or can let energies flow through us to affect physical matter, so we can increase harmony and balance by visualizing a troubled or irate person as happy and at peace within himself. Try it on the next woman you see angrily sputtering at the checkout counter in a supermarket. Visualize her as contented and loving, send her the energies, and see if she does not turn away with a smile.

If others are gossiping about the failings of someone you know, be brave enough to interject a positive thought, by speaking of that person's good qualities. This can set off a "ripple effect," of which my Walk-in friends so frequently speak. Because they brought in awareness, the Walk-ins seem intuitively to understand the principle that thoughts are things, and that by speaking kindly of another, the idea will spread to those in the gossiping circle, and through them to an ever widening group of individuals as they speak of it to others. Thus, harmony is achieved.

The Guides say of this: "Now as to ripple effect, when one's mental activities influence another, and that person another, and so on through those with whom each comes in contact, it is like casting a stone in the water and watching the circles, or ripples, become larger and larger until the entire lake may seem like a satellite of the stone cast. So it is as we influence the behavior and thoughts of others through our own activities, and why it is so important to be kind and thoughtful and loving, lest we have a deleterious effect on an entire community, or even an entire society. Walk-ins are adept at instilling confidence in others, and through this rippling effect they influence a wide range of acquaintances."

A Walk-in may quietly go about his work simply by speaking kindly of others. From there the energy can spread through a workplace or business, creating more harmonious conditions, and as each worker brings the greater harmony home with him, it spreads through his family and out to their acquaintances and friends. There is no more effective use of the energies than projecting them to others in love and harmony. The Guides say that this method could work wonders in cooling racial tensions, and preventing wars.

The most dramatic demonstration of channeled energies that I personally have experienced occurred at the close of a four-day seminar in which a group of us had been working together to experiment with largely untapped areas of the human mind. No one in the group was particularly psychic. We were simply an ordinary collection of people, and with some difficulty I had persuaded my husband to accompany me.

In the final hour, the leader, who happened to be a successful businessman from Florida, asked us to arrange our chairs in a circle and hold hands. An empty seat had been placed in the center, and as each individual in turn occupied the center chair for a minute or two, we were directed to send love and healing energies to him.

This had been quietly going on for approximately a quarter of an hour when my turn came. As I advanced toward the vacant chair, I felt a distinct electric shock and then a tingling all over, as if I were crossing through a magnetized curtain to reach the center of the circle. The prickles continued while I sat in the chair, and I felt exactly as if an electrified substance that could be touched was encircling me. It was a radiating, pulsating, physical sensation of pure love. Not until I returned to my seat in the circle did my world return to normal.

I was stunned! Had I imagined it? But that was impossible, and as no one had told us what to expect, it could not be attributed to the power of suggestion.

When the session ended, I drew my husband aside and asked if he had felt any particular sensation while taking his turn in the center of the circle. I defy anyone to produce a man or woman more practical than my husband, or less interested in psychic phenomena; yet he described exactly the same physical reactions I had experienced.

Recalling this puzzling incident to Miriam several years after the event, I sought an explanation, and the elderly Wise One commented: "The dynamic behind the experience is in the fact that mind is not brain. The brain is the biochemical, electrical switchboard that the mind uses as the link between inner being and the life form that it is occupying. When a group of three or more are in a circle, beaming the same thought toward one in the center, the minds are unwittingly letting certain powerful energies flow. It's like taking two or three batteries in a series, to step up the so-called psychic voltage. When all in a group are asked to beam something to someone, they have let their minds become channels, and the 'receiver' in the center has quite an experience. Perhaps others will try it!"

I might add here that I have sat in smaller circles and have not received a similar electrical charge. On that particular evening, when I experienced love energy as a physical reality, approximately twenty sat in the linked circle. Imagine, then, the energy toward peace that we could project if hundreds of us formed such circles simultaneously in various parts of the world!

CHAPTER XIII

Working Together

Learning to adjust to cooperative living is said to be a key to survival in the coming age, and by doing our inner homework now, we will be better equipped to meet the challenges of the next few decades.

Cooperative living does not necessarily mean living together, but rather looking out for one another and being concerned. All of us are aware of the catastrophic conditions that often result from a massive power failure in our cities, with the resultant looting and rampaging through the streets, the food spoilage, and the lack of fuel. We know what havoc can occur when an unusually heavy snow storm paralyzes traffic, halts deliveries, and blocks garbage collection. If pandemonium is created by such relatively isolated occurrences as these, it is mind-boggling to think of the worldwide chaos that could result from a shift of the axis.

Our increasingly complex society, in which everyone looks to centralized government for solutions, can suffer a complete breakdown unless we again learn the self-reliance and small-group reliance that so effectively served our early pioneers.

The way to begin is with human kindness.

A friend of mine vividly recalls an incident from her childhood that could serve as an example for all of us. While her parents were away on a business trip, she and her brother and sister were staying with her grandmother in a rather new suburban area of New York City, where the neighbors scarcely knew each other except as nodding acquaintances. On this particular day a hurricane was predicted, with high winds, heavy rains, and the possibility of a power failure. The grandmother, who had no automobile, was wondering how to protect the children in her charge, when there was a knock at the front door.

"Grandmother opened the door to find a young couple from across the street," my friend remembers. "We did not know them except by sight, but they were carrying a length of clothesline, rolls of masking tape, and a cardboard box full of candles. They asked Grandma if we needed help in tying anything down or taping the big picture windows, and if she had plenty of candles. The man walked with her around the house, noticed a frail awning, lowered it, and tied it down securely. He checked for anything else that might blow around in high winds, taped the windows, and told Grandma how to signal them if any problems should arise. Then they moved on to the next house, and the next. I have never forgotten that fine couple. They did not organize any big neighborhood effort, but they selflessly went around the immediate neighborhood making sure that everyone was secure."

Prior to the Industrial Revolution that inaugurated our current era of technological complexity, human beings tended to live more cooperatively. The small European villages where farming families for hundreds of years have clustered for safety and companionship, going out each morning to till the surrounding fields, are good examples of cooperative living. In more dangerous times, single-family units had difficulty surviving the threat of severe winters, marauding bands and highwaymen, as many of our early settlers tragically discovered, but by living closely together, groups of families could look after one another, providing safety and strength.

Extended families, such as the Irish clans and American Indian tribes, practiced a form of cooperative living; and even today in rural and semirural areas we find clusters of houses, with each young married couple building on the father's land, so that they can pool their farming efforts, raise barns, mend roofs, and look after each other.

Lacking an extended family, many people are organizing themselves into neighborhood associations or block associations in urban and suburban areas. Group members may initiate common garden projects with a common compost bin, take turns hosing off mutual sidewalks, pitch in to plant flowers that all can enjoy, and keep an eye on each other's houses when they are away. By getting to know one another, they create an environment of greater safety and caring, and will recognize a prowling stranger as one who is not from the block. In this way they decrease their dependence on police and fire protection in a system that is becoming increasingly complex and impersonal.

Another sign of our changing times is the increased use of land associations formed by several families who wish to live in a peaceful rural setting but who lack the financing to initiate such a move on their own. By pooling a portion of their resources, they can purchase a sizeable tract, reserving certain acreage for individual homes, but holding a large stretch of the open land in common.

Cooperative households have come into common vogue in the past decade, with the rising divorce rate and the increasing number of single parents. Each household sets its own rules according to the life-styles of those participating, and they pool such common responsibilities as child care, cooking, cleaning, and maintenance. Members may set rules governing meal guests, and some of them specifically bar intimacy between members of the household in order to create a more stable home situation for all. Two advantages of these cooperative households are that by pooling efforts, single parents are able to afford a nicer house in a better neighborhood for their children than a single paycheck could provide, and that way they achieve greater companionship.

Communes are a larger experiment in cooperative living. Their growth has waxed and waned throughout history, and one of the earliest American examples was the New Harmony, Indiana, community that eventually died out because all members were required to be celibate. But with the changes the Guides foresee for Planet Earth at the end of the century, communes are likely to become more popular.

Many of today's communes got off to a bad start in the 1960s, with their free life-styles, mate swapping, and drug usage; but with the passage of time many of them have settled into more stable units, with the emphasis on cooperation and harmony.

Needless to say, there are good communes and bad communes. The Guides, when asked to comment on this, wrote: "As to Findhorn, it has potential for great good in the coming stresses, and in food preparations for the war and the shift of the axis. Others of like orientation will also be attracting favorable attention, and as many communes have cleaned up their behavioral patterns and settled down to working with energies, they will attract wide acclaim in the decades ahead. As for the Moonies [followers of Korean leader Sun Myung Moon's Unification Church] and other such mind-bending cults, they are an abomination. Any justifiable group would welcome visits from parents and encourage visits by the participants to their homes, so that they could define for others the objectives of the group—not try to hide their operations and their aims. Dire and dreadful are such cults as the Moonies."

David Adler, the twenty-four-year-old Washington publisher of *Dossier* magazine, who was rescued in early 1978 by his parents from a Moonie group and has since been speaking out against the cult, classifies as equally dangerous such other sects as the Maharaj Ji's Divine Light Mission, Hare Krishna, the Children of God, Synanon, the Church of Scientology, and Jews for Jesus. He says that his own deprogramming, after only one month in a Moonie group, required six or seven months, because: "The mind is reduced to zero as a result of the brainwashing. Your ability to think is shot to pieces, and the danger can last as long as a year after you are deprogrammed."

While the writing of this book was in progress, the civilized world was horrified at news of the murders and mass suicides inspired by the Reverend Jim Jones, "father" of a cult called the People's Temple, in Jonestown, Guyana. The tragedy began with the murder of Representative Leo J. Ryan of California and three newsmen in his investigative party, followed by the mass suicide ritual in which more than nine hundred followers of Jim Jones died.

Sickened by the ghoulish tragedy, I waited three days before asking the Guides about it. Then they wrote: "They are here, alas, poor souls, in a state of shock, not realizing that they are in spirit, and waiting to be driven back to work in the fields. It is a sad commentary on the frailties of the human spirit when freedom is lacking for the minds.

The driven ones are unaware of what has occurred, and even here are trying to hide. Jones is still asleep. Ryan is awake and aware, but is not with those who took their own lives." Apparently those who committed suicide were in a different dimension.

"The fanatic cults are soul-searing," the Guides continued, "due to the denial of freedom and free will for their members. Many of these people from Guyana had as little control over their lives as if they were babies tossed on a stormy sea. Through exhaustion and brainwashing they had lost all sense of humanity or feeling, and were as menial dogs awaiting another kick or an order to be obeyed through fear. A sad, sad commentary on free Americans."

A month later, worrying about those bewildered souls, I asked the Guides for a progress report. "They are adjusting," they wrote, "and finding for themselves the evils of charismatic people who are on ego trips of their own. They are relishing the fact that so many from the Guyana establishment are here together, for they were as alike as peas in a pod in their misunderstanding of what life is all about. The ones who had higher mentality are feeling foolish at their own stupidity and are assessing the errors that led them into such a fruitless situation. The culprit Jones is still in a somnolent state, unable to understand why there is such 'misunderstanding' of his goals. He is not with the others. As we have said, not all go to the same dimension in the crossover, and his is a lowly one indeed."

I asked for further comment on so-called religious cults like those of Jim Jones, Charles Manson, and others that indulge in mind control, and the Guides replied: "They are of the devil. They are avenging, filthy, despoiled, degrading instances of the evil that man impresses on others in the name of Christianity or God. There is something so odorous about them they should be expunged from the face of the earth. These grafting egoists should not be allowed to continue their evil ways. Root them out, for they are anathema to God. We say that because there are those in higher dimensions who have a special wrath for the Jim Joneses and others who despoil God's name."

Because it is unlike the Guides to sound so vehement, I began the next morning's session by asking if they had actually written those words. After all, I consider myself an imperfect receiver, and because of my own reaction to the killings in Guyana, I thought that I might have influenced their writing. After my usual meditation, the Guides declared: "The writing of yesterday was indeed ours. Those freedom-erasing cults should be stopped as firmly as one would stop the governor of a state who decreed that all citizens must follow his personal orders—and his only—without regard to their own wishes. Those cults have nothing to do with freedom of worship.

"But these cults are not to be confused with the honorable communes and ashrams where man's aim is to seek God's will and to help others in their upward climb."

This prompted me to ask how individuals can

differentiate between a wise commune and a dangerous one. My unseen friends replied: "As to wise communes, they are those which respect each other, fairly share tasks, and give unstintingly of themselves for the good of the group. This is done with full freedom of choice, and each member is free to leave at any time that he feels out of kilter with the group, taking his earthly belongings with him. No one is required to give all that he possesses to such a group, nor is he made to sign a paper that he will forever remain. They are free individuals, joining together in common cause, but free to withdraw at any time. The group is also free to request that a member withdraw if he is not pulling his share of the load and is simply freeloading. In other words, these are people who wish to share and work together. There is no coercion. The leaders are freely selected, and although one person may have originated the idea for the commune and set it in motion, he is not a pontiff or a pope, but rather one with a solid interest in the success of the project, with the goal of helping all. Working together in harness is as old as civilized man. America was founded on this principle, as William Penn and others brought their bands of European dissidents to the New World in order to share and build together. The early American settlers sought freedom of worship, as did Martin Luther [German leader of the Protestant Reformation], who revolted against the tyranny of the medieval Roman Catholic Church."

My Walk-in friend Michael stresses that any group is only as strong as its members, and will fall apart if each of them has an individual axe to grind. "It doesn't make any difference whether it's a social, religious, business, or hobby club, a school system, or even the military," he said. "Once the individuals start to go after their individual advantage and to hell with the others, the group ceases to exist. Even Group Mind would fall apart if the individuals were not committed to working toward what is best for the Brotherhood and its goals. But when a number of individuals follow a charismatic leader, allowing themselves to be brainwashed instead of retaining their own individual conscience as to right and wrong, that leader, if he gets off balance, will destroy the group. Look at Hitler. Mussolini. Stalin. The only way they could rule was by force, fear, brutality, threats, and violence."

Michael said that a wise leader of a commune, or of any other group, is one who avoids becoming a father figure, or a power figure, and is willing to work at ordinary tasks like anyone else. "The best leadership is by example," he explained. "A good leader will not ask anyone in that group to do something he is unwilling to do if he's able. He is willing to do what he's asking others to do, and he will always give a reason why he is asking. It will be a simple, logical reason, so that others can accept it as important for the group's goal. He won't just say, 'Do this because I say so.' That's not leadership; that's autocracy.

"A good leader is willing to listen to his followers, because they may have ideas that can benefit the group. A good leader is able to plan, and is willing to disclose his plans to the group and reach a consensus in which majority opinion prevails. The one exception is the military. It has to be autocratic because the military exists for the sole purpose of fighting and winning battles, and the safety of the group depends on the obedience of each person within it."

Because the dire events in Guyana tend to make us look upon all cults or religious communes as potentially dangerous, I asked Michael how a sincere seeker could delineate the good groups from the bad ones. This is his reply: "Before joining I would watch the group to see what the stated goals are, why it was formed, and what purposes it intends to serve. Then, in light of its stated purposes and goals, I would look to see how well the individuals were hewing to those precepts. I would next study the leadership of the group, to see if it was sincerely committed to those goals, or whether the leaders were on an ego trip and using the efforts of others for their own personal benefit. Are the leaders willing to listen to the followers? Is the group self-governing? Do the members work willingly with their leadership or have the power to replace it if they are dissatisfied? If individuals within a group are denied the right to think for themselves and make suggestions for improvements, they are being brainwashed, and I would have nothing to do with it. But if they are quietly working together to make themselves more self-reliant and less dependent on today's complex social structure, that is good, and you're going to see a great deal more of that in the decades ahead."

As Michael sees it, cooperative households for broken family units who pool a portion of their incomes in order to provide themselves and their children with more attractive quarters than they could otherwise afford are a first step in discovering the advantages and disadvantages of cooperative living. He calls it basic training at the grassroots level, and observes: "This is just the blades of grass springing up, before you have a complete lawn. They are getting experience, seeing what works and what doesn't work, so that in a time of crisis they are better prepared for survival. In our present state of technology it is possible for individuals and pairs to live off by themselves, but in a time of real crisis the system will break down. Even the distribution and transportation systems could collapse, and if people are without basic skills, and without knowledge of how to work together, they may not survive."

I asked Michael what Walk-ins are doing to help others prepare for such a contingency, and he replied: "They are sowing seeds, trying to get people to accept one another as fellow human beings and to work together in small groups. All that most of the Walk-ins can do right now is plant the ideas and encourage others to try them out. If people will work together now in neighborhood groups or cooperative ventures, they will know what is viable and what to avoid when the time comes to work with larger groups."

If I interpret Michael's meaning correctly, he is saying that Walk-ins are quietly encouraging harmony between individuals and within groups, helping them to learn how to be useful and co-operative, for the betterment of mankind.

The trend in large cities today is toward condominiums and cooperative apartments. Bob and I, after more than thirty years of owning the individual houses in which we lived, recently bought a cooperative apartment, and we are aware of the advantages and disadvantages of both life-styles. Jointly owned buildings are a different kettle of fish from rental apartments, since the shareholders, or owners, of individual units must work together in maintaining the building, keeping down expenses, handling the personnel, and enforcing the rules that ensure privacy and a pleasant home atmosphere. There is also the problem of dealing with those few occupants who refuse to cooperate.

The Guides, in commenting on these changing life-styles, declared: "There are benefits and drawbacks to both ways of living, and it is for each to decide. While a person is reasonably strong and independent, there is advantage to living in a separate dwelling with one's own family, but as he reaches the age of ailments and frailties it is better to live in a cooperative way, and for this reason many are choosing that method. This is not the only benefit, for in learning to cooperate with one another and helping others over rough periods, people are increasing their own opportunities for service and soul advancement. The communes are fashioned to pool the efforts of those still in their physical prime, so that by helping each other they are also benefited by a good life-style that suits their needs. Surrendering independence is one of

the most difficult things to learn, and it is therefore important to give a great deal of thought to
it, before joining a commune or a community of
pooled interests. In a survival situation it is necessary, and if one has already learned how to conduct himself in such a working arrangement, it
is all to the good. But remember, freedom of individual thought is paramount, and one must retain his right to leave a group."

Perhaps Michael best sums up what the Guides
are talking about when he says: "All humanity on
this planet, regardless of color, creed, race, sex, or
nationality is one family. All human beings are
brothers. They're all one being. Every human
being is on this planet to learn. No one is here for
a free ride. Everyone chose to come here, to wear
a human life form in order to learn something that
he knew he needed to learn. Unfortunately, people
sometimes forget that they're simply 'wearing'
their bodies. They get hung up in the illusion they
call the real world."

CHAPTER XIV

The Flames of War

The nuclear war! The needless war of the 1980s that can still be avoided if we learn to live cooperatively with one another, put ourselves in the Flow, and send forth the energies toward peace.

Unfortunately, the Guides see little possibility of that idyllic state being achieved in time to prevent the holocaust of World War III.

The Horn of Africa, they say, is the place to watch. If they are correct in their prognostications, World War III will be set off around 1986 by Ethiopia, which will first subvert and then attack some of its neighbors. The conflagration will "spread like the proverbial wildfire" throughout the troubled continent of Africa, eventually engulfing most of the nations of the earth in the flames of war.

The Guides say of the two decades remaining in this century: "The shift of the axis is unavoidable, and the world will be better off after it has thus been cleansed. But the war is another matter. It is within the realm of man's ingenuity to avoid it, since man has free will in his own conduct, but the forces now in operation will have to be reversed if it is to be stopped before it starts. All conflicts are avoidable if enough souls pray together for peace, and love one another. Thus, the war need not be waged, but it is unlikely to be averted if the present course continues."

The wheels, they say, have already been set in motion. During the past year, Ethiopia's Marxist military rulers have bombed neighboring Somalia and fought bloody battles in the breakaway province of Eritrea with the aid of Russian-made MIG bombers, Soviet tanks, and Cuban soldiers. Soviet-armed Vietnam has toppled the government of Chinese-backed Cambodia, and in retaliation China has invaded Vietnam, with widespread killing. Dictator Idi Amin's Uganda forces have seized a large chunk of Tanzania, and many more bloody confrontations will occur along the frontiers in the Middle East and Asia before the year is out.

These are only the prologue. As the Guides see it, the first half of the 1980s will follow much the same pattern as the 1970s, with border skirmishes in the Middle East and Africa, Latin America, and the Far East. Then, shortly after the halfway mark of the decade is passed, the "real conflagration" will begin, with violent fighting erupting in the area of Ethiopia.

As long ago as 1973, the Guides began telling me about a then obscure "man of mixed lineage" in Abyssinia (the former name of Ethiopia which the Guides still use) who would become a very real threat to world peace. In 1975–76, while dictating much of the material for *The World Before,* they continued to harp on this man, warning that he was secretly in touch with the Kremlin hierarchy, that he was determined to seize control of Ethiopia, "and from there to wreak havoc on the surrounding area, take over oil and mineral resources, and wage war on the world."

I quoted that passage in the book, and this further comment about the Abyssinian: "His purpose is to seek world domination through anarchy and strife. He is a real menace and should be apprehended before inestimable damage is done. This devious plot will otherwise take place within the next twelve years and could trigger World War III, for the man is a dangerous fanatic. We see his plans evolving and do not want them to come to fruition."

Since then, the Guides have repeatedly cautioned me about the Abyssinian, but since his name was not divulged, and I have no influence in our government, I paid little heed to their warnings.

Then, in November 1978, they declared that the man about whom they had been writing had just signed a treaty of friendship with the Soviet Union in Moscow. They identified him as Ethiopian strongman Mengistu Haile Mariam, a member of the Dergue (military junta) that overthrew King

Haile Selassie in 1974. Mengistu immediately became vice-chairman of the Dergue and three years later succeeded to the top post when the chairman was murdered. After learning his name, I interviewed a top source in the U.S. government, who described Mengistu Haile Mariam to me as a "fanatic" of "murky lineage," whose mother belonged to the Galla tribe, and whose father's identity is unknown, at least in America. He said that Mengistu, as a youth, attended a military school in Ethiopia maintained for those of poor background, that he twice came to America for training, and was a low-ranking officer in the Ethiopian army at the time of the coup d'etat which overthrew King Haile Selassie. He is now thirty-eight years old.

A Washington *Post* article in November 1978, reporting on the signing of the treaty between President Leonid Brezhnev of the USSR and Mengistu, stated that it was "thought to pledge long-term support by the Kremlin for its ally in the Horn of Africa." It added: "The Soviets began two years ago to provide military aid for Ethiopia in its war with Somali-backed guerrillas in the Ogaden region of the Horn." The Guides say that Mengistu will be busily subverting neighboring countries to communism during the first half of the approaching decade, in readiness for his all-out attack later on.

One reason why I am inclined to give credence to such warnings from the Guides is because they informed me, in the spring of 1976, that Teng Hsiao-ping would before long become the leader

of the People's Republic of China. Shortly thereafter, however, Chinese Premier Chou En-lai died,
Hua Kuo-feng was named to succeed him, and
Vice-Premier Teng Hsiao-ping was purged. With
some asperity I pointed this out to the Guides, but
in their unflappable way they responded that Teng
would regain power after the death of Chairman
Mao Tse-tung.

"Although his power will be of fairly short du-
ration in China," I quoted them in *The World
Before,* "Teng will cooperate with the West to a
greater degree than Mao, and will begin the process of returning China to the world of friendly
nations."

That prophetic utterance sounded ridiculous
three years ago, but no one presently doubts that
Vice-Premier Teng Hsiao-ping is the real strongman of Red China. *Time* magazine has named him
Man of the Year, and although Hua still has the
title of premier, Teng has told visiting dignitaries
that he himself declined the offer of the premier-
ship following the death of Mao. Certainly he has
opened China's long-closed gates to the modern
world, admitting more than a half-million tourists
during 1978, and making numerous personal trips
abroad, including a widely publicized one to the
United States. Ten thousand Chinese students are
being sent to the West to learn languages, technology, and science, and Teng is launching a vast
modernization program with billions of dollars'
worth of purchases from Japan and the West.

Because the Guides have proven so right about
Teng, who stunningly leaped to the top after his

purge by the "Gang of Four," I believe that careful heed should be paid to their warnings about Mengistu and Ethiopia.

It is a rather gloomy picture that the Guides are painting for the decade ahead. At the time that I was preparing the manuscript for this book, they predicted that President Carter would be succeeded in the White House by another Democrat, who would surround himself with capable advisors, but would pour so much of the nation's wealth into welfare and health insurance programs that the heavily burdened middle class would "virtually take up arms because of high taxation."

However, Republican Ronald Reagan succeeded Carter, and immediately began the herculean task of trying to cut back Big Government and big spending. When I asked the Guides for an explanation of their error, they reminded me of what they had previously written concerning the possibility of World War III. Man has free will, they emphasized, and enough Americans switched party loyalties in the last week or ten days before the 1980 election to confound the pollsters.

"As to Reagan succeeding Carter, it was there all the time for us to see," they wrote, "but we inadvertently looked too far ahead, since we were viewing the next two decades as a whole. We foresaw the results of a big-spending Democratic president who will nearly bankrupt the American economy, but that is to occur after Reagan's one term in the White House, unless the voters again exercise free will by preventing this fiscal irresponsibility. The Soviets, taking advantage of the perilous situation in the United States, will otherwise encroach in Africa and the Middle East, seizing oil in the producing nations, and creating havoc throughout that area of the world."

My unseen friends say that this big-spending future Democratic president will not be Senator Ted Kennedy, former Vice President Walter Mondale, or Governor Jerry Brown. Of the latter they said enigmatically, "He is a stranger on this earth, and not quite of it. He will gradually fade from the picture, and will eventually go into a monastery, or the Eastern equivalent thereof."

Trying to postpone a discussion of World War III as long as possible, I asked the Guides to comment on the early part of the decade, and they replied: "The English economy will continue to improve for a while, thanks in part to the North Sea oil deposits, but these will begin to run out within the next ten years, and as the Tories will be in power, they will institute measures for the encouragement of business so that jobs are provided and good housing assured. The United States, running in the opposite direction, will pour billions into wasteful welfare projects, and discourage production through laws that make it impractical to expand and develop and earn. Germany will remain strong, and France will have its ups and downs, with Communists moving toward positions of power. Italy is in a dangerous decline. Saudi Arabia will skid downhill as oil production lags. Solar energy will move to the forefront, with a revolutionary new means of entrapping solar rays. South America will be turbulent, and the Panama Canal will fail to serve the needs of the United States when war erupts."

The Guides said there will be continuing inflation, "but not the runaway variety that so hampered Germany and China before World War II." The oil-producing nations, they added, "will for a time curb their appetites and sell their product at somewhere approaching the current inflated prices, which will give time for scientists to develop workable substitutes for oil as energy."

Well before Iran deposed the Shah as its ruler, the Guides foresaw the event and said that he would never return to power. At that time they saw him eventually settling in Europe, and after his demise much later they wrote: "The Shah was not fore-ordained to pass into spirit when he did, but he had lost his will to live. Cancer and many other diseases are as much the result of mental attitudes as physical disabilities, and because he felt betrayed by the Carter administration and other so-called Free World powers, he no longer desired to live as a has-been."

The Guides predict that large-scale crop failures will contribute to the tensions of the early 1980s. "The threat of famine will commence in Russia," they declared, "and the rest of the world will be hard-pressed to meet its needs. The Chinese will also have food shortages on a vast scale, and the entire ring of Northern Hemisphere nations, including Canada, will suffer from the failure of crops. Entreaties for food shipments abroad will shoot up domestic prices, provoking riots in the United States and elsewhere. Since hunger produces rioting faster than anything else, nations should now be storing food against the lean years. The requirement for food will set off fighting by those have-nots who want to be haves, and Ethiopia will be the worst offender."

Disturbed by their dire forebodings, I asked if there is any other means except "prayer and love" for averting World War III, and the Guides replied: "Those who direct the war machines are the culprits, and to continue selling arms, munitions, and killer-planes to underdeveloped countries is a part of the horrendous reality. Let those who would arm neighbor against neighbor heed these warnings, for it is as wrong to provide the wherewithall as it is to explode the actual missiles. This, then, is our message: Stop the arms traffic."

I wanted to know if it is wrong for us to arm defensively, and they declared: "It is the only way, for what will happen if the enemies are so strong that they can overrun a nation that has stood firmly for human rights and the dignity of the individual soul? Do not let down the defenses. Keep so strong that all will fear to trespass, or to begin the nuclear warfare that will so decimate the population that the shift of the axis will seem almost peaceful by contrast. Be loving, temperate in word and deed, and ease world tensions, but do not feel that America must be in the middle of every dispute and every move toward coexistence. Let others find their steps toward peace, without always being in the center of the controversy.

"We see the clouds of war hovering over the face of the earth," the Guides continued. "Unless forces for peace become so strong as to make it impossible, there will be violent uprisings, with nuclear explosions in the skies and underfoot. There will be chaos, and some will be happy to leave their physical bodies."

Recalling that in an earlier book the Guides said victims of Europe's Hundred Years' War were returning to earth to try to prevent World War III, or to refuse to fight in it, I asked for an update, and they replied that many of them will be at, or nearing, draft age in the mid-1980s. "When man refuses to fight, and lays down his arms," they wrote, "he is less a coward than those who push the buttons of war and tell others to fight the battles. Those in authority are greater cowards than the lowly foot soldier who simply says, 'No, thank you,' and stops fighting. Some of the worst wars in history have been fought under the guise of patriotism, but what is patriotism? Little more than defense of one's homeland from foreign aggressors. It is not pertinent when vast armies are shipped abroad to interfere in someone else's quarrel."

The Guides say that those who would avert the catastrophe of war should begin now to preach dispassionate love for their fellowmen. "The Walk-ins are quietly spreading the word that all men are entitled to freedom of choice and of mind, and that none should impose his own beliefs and governmental policies on another people," they declared. "Some of these Walk-ins are in reasonably high places within governments, and are therefore given some voice, but thus far they are too few to have a real impact. That is why there are so many more returning to adult bodies as rapidly as vehicles become available, to try to prevent the catastrophes that are otherwise almost sure to come. Man will have to change within himself, not try to change others, in order to prevent wars."

The Guides foresee that as border skirmishes of the early 1980s become more heated, with one nation after another battling its neighbors, "the United States will be torn into factions, as it sees its friends mauled by their enemies, while the United Nations talks endlessly, without taking action.

"There will be a war party in the United States, small but strident, wanting to send arms to the invaded countries," they continued, "but others will recall Vietnam and demand that nothing be done. There will be some who sincerely believe that by stepping in, a larger war will be averted, but others will insist that the United States remain free from entanglement. As the decade nears its halfway mark, there will be more strident calls for United Nations action, and Europe will fear for its safety. In the Far East, some nations will seek aid from Russia and others from the United States, but the economy of the latter will be too beset for it to do more than issue warnings."

The Guides say that the kickoff for World War III will occur about 1986 when Ethiopia launches a military offensive against its neighbors. "Backed by Soviet armaments, it will quickly ignite that entire area of Africa, and the fighting will spread out like tentacles across the seas," they warned.

"The Chinese will call for help, and as the trouble worsens there will be fighting in the area of Iran and Turkey, with Soviet-dominated political parties crying for vengeance. The present Egyptian peace offensive will hold for a time, but an ultimatum from Israel will create violent reactions throughout the Arab states, setting off a round of fighting, and Egypt will go with her Arab brothers. Russia will arm the Arabs, with the United States and England backing Israel. Iran will hold out for a time, but the pressure from Soviet forces just across the border will topple the government, and, as the Middle East erupts, Russia will become more overt in its subversive activities.

"Western Europe will become alarmed, but with no stomach for fighting will hold back while its Eastern neighbors mobilize. The United Nations will become a forum for angry words by worried statesmen, but will be powerless to stop the course of violence. The U.S. President at that time will be struggling with a runaway economy and with war-sick countrymen who want no part of the battle. In China there will be a new group of leaders who will sit back to see how the cookie crumbles, and as Abyssinia rampages through Africa, Albania will struggle to remain out of the Eastern European armaments race, hoping that China will rescue it from the dilemma."

The Guides foresee that as Russia openly enters the worsening conflict, France will try desperately to protect itself from involvement, "but how can it, when it sits astride the passage from north to south and east to west in Europe?" They say that

Turkey will be forced to side with Russia, and that China will eventually be drawn in on the side of the Western allies. "America will no longer be able to sit on the fence. England will be frantically calling for aid, and despite America's rampant inflation there will be a call for a fast armament buildup. Many people will react angrily, and as the new D-Day approaches there will be dissension and divisiveness within the ranks of the people.

"This will be a time to test men's souls," the Guides predicted. "When the United States is finally forced into action after the invasion of Western Europe, it will be too late. Russia will sweep across from Eastern Europe into Paris, and the English Channel will be clogged with refugees. Great Britain, although economically more sound than the United States at that time, will be unable to support them and the turning point will come when Red Chinese forces move against Russia on its eastern flank. The turmoil will meanwhile have spread to other areas, with uprisings in Latin America and some parts of Asia."

Shivering at the dire prospects, I asked about nuclear warfare, and the Guides replied: "The Russians and the United States will use types of nuclear weapons, as will China and England, but this will not be an all-out nuclear holocaust, as many have feared. Reason, to that extent, will prevail."

Hoping for a more cheerful note, I prodded the Guides to disclose how the fighting would at last wind down. At this, they raised the twin specters of famine and storm.

"There will be famine in many of the areas overrun by war," they reported gloomily, "and nuclear explosions will poison much of the growing foods. Animals will die, and because man has become dependent on meat in many parts of the world, there will be real hardships for civilians as well as the military. Food riots in cities will become a common occurrence, and in the countrysides where fighting has raged, nutrition will be a tremendous problem. Some nuclear weaponry will produce sterile ground, and so it will worsen. The storm of the late 1980s will spread such devastation that war-weary nations, forced to repair damage and provide shelter for their people, will gradually ease off the deliberate killings, and in the early 1990s a tenuous peace will reign, except for sporadic border skirmishes."

Dreading still further disclosures, but feeling that a good reporter should ask, I dared to query them about the storm. This is their response: "A storm of unparalleled violence will sweep the Western Hemisphere, ripping out sections of the earth itself, and altering surface areas of the western United States. Some of California will go into the sea, as we have previously foretold, and damage will be unprecedented in the Western world, for it will not be confined solely to the American West. New York will suffer tremendous property loss, as will England, Norway, and other parts of Western Europe. This will be brought about by natural forces, as the earth is buffeted by intrastellar forces. It will have a disastrous effect on civilians, who are so afraid of anything they do not understand. It will seem as a curse from God on the escalating war. Many of those reincarnated victims of the Hundred Years' War will, meanwhile, have been refusing to fight, preferring death before a firing squad to taking the lives of others. This will have a profound effect on the war's ending, since the storm will remind others, too, that God can be angered by mankind."

Begging to know the conclusion, I also asked about Germany's role in the war, and my unseen friends wrote: "The Germans will be with the West and will try to protect France, but the Russians, with their satellite armies, will sweep into Paris. The French will eventually emerge free, for after China moves against Russia the troops will be spread too thinly in France, and the threat to England will also subside. There is no way for communism to take over the world. It is too limiting in human freedom, so there will be sufficient force to withstand it, and after the storm the Russians and Chinese will be occupied in fighting each other to something of a draw."

The Guides added that the shift of the axis at the close of the 1990s will eradicate mind control and closed societies within nations, because all peoples will be working together for survival.

They ended their discussion of the war by declaring: "This is as much as we wish to tell you now about those perilous times. But remember this! If men will see the folly of their ways, this war may yet be averted."

CHAPTER XV

Preparations for Safety

I was astonished one morning to read what the Guides had just written. Walk-ins, they declared, are now beginning to arrive at the rate of a thousand a week, to cope with the difficult era ahead.

A thousand a week! On succeeding mornings I queried them closely about that figure, thinking that they must have intended to say a year, or even a month, but the Guides were adamant. The tempo, they said, has considerably stepped up even during the writing of this book. I asked what percentage of the Walk-ins were Americans, and they replied that approximately ten percent are English-speaking—Americans, Canadians, and British who have taken over unwanted bodies.

Then they made another electrifying statement: "There will be a President of the United States in the latter part of this century who is a Walk-in, and he will be of inestimable value in preparing for the shift of the axis, taking precautionary measures to store records, readying safe quarters for officialdom, and directing others to areas that he will realize are to be saved from destruction.

"Another such Walk-in will preside over the French economy in that period after the war," they continued, "and these are only a few of the positions of leadership to be filled by Walk-ins."

Intrigued by the prospect, I nevertheless asked my unseen friends if there might be danger in revealing their prediction at this time. Would some of our citizens be fearful of having a Walk-in for a President, and try to defeat him?

Not at all, they replied, adding: "Walk-ins by then will be so greatly admired that there will be no harm in stating that the President will be one. This is not necessarily a criterion for campaigning for office, but there will be ways to recognize which is the right candidate, with the finest abilities for seeing America through the aftermath of the war and the perilous nineties."

The time is not far off, they declared, when those who are accustomed to thinking only of themselves will begin to feel an out-flowing of love for others, as they work together for the common good. "The war will provide the groundwork, since many will share the same problems then, and will feel a oneness that has been absent among human beings for a long time. There are those among them who will rise to leadership, and some of them will be Walk-ins who understand the principles of unity, and will demonstrate it to those around them."

The Guides said that Walk-ins will be arriving at an even faster pace during the war of the late 1980s, taking the bodies of injured or deserting soldiers who have lost the will to live. "They will try to move those who will listen to safer areas, and will prepare shelters for the sick and the homeless. They are studying now for this reformation of logistics and advance planning, and will be heard from to a larger extent as the nineteen eighties pass."

My unseen pen pals have repeatedly stressed that inner preparation is our most pressing challenge. "The time ahead is one of self-searching rather than self-seeking," they admonished. "The next two decades are in many ways the most crucial ever to confront the modern world. They will be times of sorrow and suffering, but they will also offer joy—the greatest opportunity in two thousand years for man to find himself and his relationship with the Creator. Adversities offer more opportunities for soul growth than easy or opulent times. Our fiber is strengthened by the crosses that we have to bear, and even as we overcome these hurdles we are growing and flowering. If we, through gallant exercise of our talents and character, surmount these obstacles, the road ahead should be a welcome one. Let no man fear the decades of the eighties and nineties, if, like the Christian knights of old, he is ready to do battle with evil. Seldom is such opportunity available for soul growth as these two decades before the turn of the century."

The Guides say that millions of earthlings will survive the shift in physical body. "Material attachments are fragmentary at best," they counseled, "and none will feel regret who has prepared himself for this alteration of the earth's surface. True, what you earthlings term civilization will diminish as the earth changes wipe out the hydroelectric plants, the housing developments, the palaces, and the tenements, but these are illusory, for does not the Bible promise that there are mansions in heaven for all who aspire to rightdoing?"

According to the Guides, the Walk-ins are "well aware of the coming shift," and many of them are quietly organizing, with Brotherhood members, small groups to cope with the threatened chaos. "Some are seeding ideas, and others seeding grounds which they sense will be safe areas of the world. They are planting fruit and nut trees, and will be storing grain against future needs. Some will be delving into the logistic problems for enabling those who wish to survive to be transported to safety. Certain groups are praying steadily to prevent war and find ways to implant peace in men's hearts. When the time is ripe, they will mobilize in peaceful conclaves to spread faith and hope and charity, for all those will be needed to see men through the debacle of the eighties and the changes of the nineties. Some Walk-ins will soothe inner fears, while others prepare people for rapid harvesting of grains and weaving of protective covering from basic substances, even straw.

Some are already teaching basic skills, and some will be storing documents in safe places. There *will* be safe areas, you know! And as the time approaches, these will be made known through Brotherhoods and inner awareness so that those wishing to survive in physical being will be aided in going there."

Since the Guides had written that there will be safe areas, I asked if they would identify some of them for people who wish to move there now. "There will be some clues to safe areas if one will heed his intuition," they replied, "but we are not going to pinpoint areas for people to flee to at this time. There is no point in doing so. Naming them now would cause the misfits and unharmonious ones to flock there, whereas the good-at-heart would be too sensible to disrupt their households by moving there now. There is plenty of time, and those who would learn to heed their intuition will feel the rightness of their moves in the 1990s."

I wondered how Walk-ins would be able to convince people of the need for preparation when the time approaches, and the Guides responded: "They will find some listeners among scientists, who will begin to see signs of an approaching slippage of the earth. The weather will have worsened in most areas, and the Brotherhoods and Walk-ins who psychically receive knowledge from this side will begin to enumerate areas that will survive virtually intact, although with some climatic changes. These will mostly be inland, away from the ferocity of the seas: and valleys between rolling hills will have protection from the high gale winds that will sweep across open places. Seeds will be especially developed to withstand abrupt changes of temperature and buffeting by the winds. These will be lowlying varieties that have tenacious roots, and, of course, there are the underground foods such as potatoes, onions, and turnips."

As the Guides see it, preparations now under way to store microfilm and other valuables beneath the surface of the earth are "steps in the right direction, although some of the storage areas being prepared deep in the earth's crust will be under water for thousands of years after the shift." They said that as the world pulls itself together following the war, Walk-ins will encourage the storage of documents, microfilm, and tapes "in such safe areas as the heartland of countries away from the sea, and in mountainous caves in the Rockies, the Appalachians, and the Alps," and that it is not too soon to begin preparing such places.

Disturbed that the Guides' warnings might unnecessarily upset readers of the book, I asked Miriam what I could do to erase that fear. In her sagacious way, she responded: "Fear is not erased. Fear is dealt with, with courage. As President Roosevelt once said, 'The only thing to fear is fear itself.' When you realize that it's the fears that are making mountains out of molehills, and you look at the problem courageously, all of a sudden the mountains dissipate and you see them for what they are—molehills. Most human beings fear death, because to them what is beyond death is an unknown. Actually, they fear the unknown. When more people come to understand that death is merely transition into a greater freedom, they will fear it less."

The Guides, in commenting on that statement, said: "Why do souls in physical bodies regret leaving them for a better spirit life? Solely due to their unawareness of the greater opportunity here for freedom and happiness. The Church has had much to do with this situation, with its dire preachings of hell-fire and damnation, and so have the old wives' tales of sleeping in the cold earth until judgment day, or of frightening apparitions that allegedly wander in the night. All are so false as to be degrading even to contemplate. All will live on, in self-judgment and greater striving for good, until the time when we are reunited with our Creator. Remember, a soul is imperishable, and no matter what occurs in the physical plane, the real *you* survives."

Stressing again the need for inner preparation, and the importance of learning to love selflessly, the Guides said that when the sudden shift occurs, "some will ascend quickly to higher realms in the spirit world, having conquered old fears and ancient hatreds, whereas others will remain earthbound, seething with resentments which had best be left in the physical world and not carried forward.

"Some will decide to take on new projects here, but some will sit back and remonstrate with fate, not realizing that we are the masters of our own fate from one lifetime to another," they continued. "Help us to spread the message that if all those who heed the warning will commence at once to project love instead of self-interest, there will be more spiritual gains for more souls in these next two decades than in all of recorded history. The next twenty years are crucial to the unfolding of a soul's spiritual being, for unless mankind uses these years to smooth out past karma and prepare for the spirit state, the opportunities may not come again for thousands of years, inasmuch as the human population will be decimated and opportunities for entering physical bodies will be slim. Those who strive now to complete their rehabilitation will advance more rapidly in spirit, to compensate for the lost opportunities in the earth life."

Walk-ins, by retaining awareness, intuitively realize that death is not to be feared, and that loving one another is vital to a soul's progress. Although they do not preach to others, they are able to spread the message through quiet example, which ripples out in widening circles. By remaining in the Flow and encouraging people to follow their own inner guidance, they will help them to relocate in safe places if they wish to survive the shift. The Guides stress that not everyone will want to survive in human body, but that for those who do, it will be an interesting and fascinating era, full of challenges and opportunities.

Many of the messages that we have already reported from Walk-ins and the Guides are basically tools for survival in the two decades ahead: using the energies, manifesting needed objects, loving unselfishly, learning self-reliance through basic skills, living in harmony with one another, listening to one's inner guidance, maintaining good health, and becoming a part of the Flow.

Since these abilities are not easily acquired in a time of grave crisis, they say that it is wise to begin testing them now, while there is still time. If we have learned to rely on our inner wisdom, while putting ourselves into the Flow, we will intuitively know where to locate and how to prepare, so that we will be in a stronger position to ride the waves of change.

Walk-ins are said to be working at all levels to foster self-reliance by encouraging efforts to grow food, spreading an awareness of the frailty of our energy and supply networks, teaching youngsters how to camp out safely in all kinds of weather, learning which wild plants are edible, and how to start root cellars that will keep carrots, turnips, potatoes, onions, and cabbages fresh for many months.

Acquiring skills that we can share or barter with others is especially valuable preparation. Miriam says of this: "Each person will be inclined in a different direction, according to his own interest, and in a chaotic time they will be able to pool their knowledge." She said that Walk-ins are quietly encouraging this trend, and that while some are learning proper use of the soil, others are acquiring medical training or midwifery skills, learning how to work with fabrics, leather, and skins, developing herb gardens, drying fruits and vegetables for preservation, fashioning pottery from local clay, and discovering how to harness water power to run machines without electricity.

"Everyone who wants to survive would do well to learn a few basic skills that can be shared," she cautioned. "They would also be wise to gather such simple equipment as needles, sharpening stones, knives, axes, fish hooks, hammers, and other hand tools that are not electrically operated."

According to Michael, a number of cooperative groups and communes have formed because the members know that a major change is to occur on Planet Earth. "They may not talk about this aspect of it, to avoid ridicule, just as Noah was ridiculed while building his Ark," he said with a grin, "but they know what they're doing. They are listening to their inner direction, and although Walk-ins are not members of the communes, some of us are giving them encouragement from the sidelines. These people, by learning now what will work and what won't, will have valuable contributions to make in the days ahead."

Michael said that not least among the things the cooperatives are learning is how to deal with freeloaders, "because there will be plenty of those around who will try to sponge off the ones that made the proper preparations." He recalled the ancient Oriental tale about a beggar who cadged fish from a fisherman, and within a few days was as hungry as before. But when he appealed for food to a second fisherman, he was invited aboard the boat, handed a fishing pole, and taught how to use it. After the beggar had caught three fish he tried to return the pole, but the wise fisherman said, "No, the pole, the line, the hooks, and bait are yours, as are the fish you caught. Now, go your way in peace." The moral would seem to be that if freeloaders try to attach themselves to those who have worked and prepared, they should be put to work or sent on their way.

Laura stresses that "hoarding five years' supply of food" is not the way to prepare. Hungry throngs will kill to get it, and he who tries to protect his supply, but is without friends, has no chance of survival in a crisis. If he has learned no basic skills, he could not even construct a hovel for protection against cold, or replace the clothing he wears on his back.

CHAPTER XVI

The Antichrist

The Guides do not often contradict themselves, but shortly after publication of *The World Before,* in 1976, they began writing rather frequently about the Antichrist, and referring to him as a schoolboy now incarnate. I had quoted them in that book as saying that the Antichrist would soon be born, and since even a "schoolboy" has a better grasp of mathematics than that, I challenged them about their previous statement.

"It was an error in transmission," they replied calmly. "You were being an imperfect receiver that day, but we should have caught and corrected that mistake before the book went to press. The one who will pretend to be the Christ had already been born in [here they named an Eastern seaboard state], and he presently resides in a Maryland suburb of Washington, D.C. A schoolboy now, he is handsome, gregarious, and well liked by his friends. His parents are attractive, well-bred people, and his father is a lawyer."

Mollified, I asked for more information about the alleged Antichrist, and they declared: "As the boy develops, he will become intensely interested in leadership, and will rise rapidly in the government. There is no reason to believe that he knows his own true identity at this time, but he is tremendously ambitious, and will do well in the university. We can tell you that shortly before the shift of the axis, he will have become so popular that people will readily follow him, as he speaks of the approaching chaos. They will harken to his instructions, and when the shift occurs many of those who survive will hail him as a prophet and savior who prepared them for the impending shift.

"There are those who will try to sound a warning, for he will be glib and egotistical; but others will say that he deserves leadership, and his fame will spread to other areas of the world, so that for a time he will seem to be the promised savior. His strength will lie in his charismatic leadership qualities, for except to those who know him well, he will exhibit a side of his nature that indeed seems benevolent. As he seizes world power there will be some awesome days, before those working through the Brotherhoods and with the Walk-ins will finally put him down."

Another time, the Guides said: "The Antichrist will be attracting attention toward the end of the century, when he is in his late twenties. He will be dynamic and inspiring of trust, in a different way than the youthful radical leaders of the 1960s. He will be clean-cut and forceful, attractive and respectable, and will fool the old as well as the young. When the shift comes, he will be preaching the wisdom of 'getting right with God,' and some who have never before given thought to the end of life will find themselves spellbound by his oratory, and want to follow his leadership. In that time of emergency he will be as one crying in the wilderness to save one's soul by following him as the new Messiah. It is an age-old cry for salvation, and this man who thwarted the Christ before, will again be teaching that he himself is the true savior."

The Guides said that when this young man completes his university studies, he will enter government service. "As to his occupation, he will direct others in an undertaking to establish controls over occupational behaviorism. As time passes, he will emerge as a front-page personality, often interviewed by the press, and he will take on other duties as a free-lance psychologist. His will be a remarkable career in that he will be studying behavioral patterns and thought processes, and after World War III he will begin to emerge as a national figure who is able to direct masses of people.

"At the close of the century he will be ready to assume world management. The shift of the axis is made to order for his directorial powers. That is why he returned at this particular time, and his charisma will enhance his acceptability. For the first two decades of the twenty-first century he will seemingly have no peer. When the time is ripe he will declare himself as the anointed one who is to lead people back to God. But that he is not, for when the Scriptures are studied, it will be seen that before that event will first come the Antichrist."

Troubled by their firm assertions, I asked what role the Walk-ins and Brotherhoods would play in dealing with the Antichrist. They replied: "The Walk-ins are warily regarding the approach of the time when the Antichrist will begin his work, for they are aware that he is already in physical being and that he will do great harm. They are not yet positive of his identity, and some are searching for him now. They will find him at least by 1990, for by then he will have begun to create a stir, with his attractive mien and his declarations of piety. The Brotherhoods are not eager to take on the task of exposing this lad, who will make trouble for all who speak out against him. They do not fear for themselves, but for the effect that it will have on those who react with horror to any criticism of the Antichrist, whom they will consider the Messiah. The Brotherhoods are in touch with each other on this point now, to the extent that they want to handle the situation without alarming the public."

When I relayed this startling message to my Walk-in friend Michael, who taps into the Group Mind of his Brotherhood, he replied: "The Guides are right on! Their information is correct."

After rereading a rather bulky file on all that

the Guides have written about the alleged Antichrist in recent years, I commenced a morning session by asking: "Will this present schoolboy do evil things when he assumes world power? If what you say about him now is true, he doesn't sound too bad. How will he die?"

Following my meditation, they responded: "The Antichrist will be the embodiment of all evil when he begins to realize his identity. Until then, he is a harmless enough lad, although he is already nurturing ambitions to rule the world. When he reaches maturity his aims will begin to frighten some others, since his unquenchable ambition for world domination is as unnatural in an American as it was in a Hitler or a Stalin. This man will play on people's emotions like a maestro on violin strings, and as the shift nears it will seem made to order for his ambitions. Realizing how frightened people will be of anything that seems like God's anger at man, he will seize the cloak of divinity, claiming that he is the anointed son returned to rescue mankind from evil. After the shift, so many will be fearful of God's wrath that they will bend to his will, while he harasses and tortures those who would speak out against him. Eventually, he will be put to death, when enough people realize the demagogic nature of his work and the selfishness of his goals. After that will come the Christ."

I asked how he will become so powerful after the shift, when that time has been prophesied as the dawning of the New Age. How will he fool so many people?

"The Antichrist will become world ruler in the sense that he will handle the guidelines and direct those who will carry out his orders," the Guides replied. "Rather than elective, these offices will be appointive, and within the network will be spies who probe into the personal lives of people during that reconstruction era. They will also be searching for the hidden records of the past, and trying to harness solar power for heating and cooling, in a world almost without oil or gas. His managerial powers at first will seem God-sent, but as he becomes more ambitious still, he will demand worshipful obedience, and in pretending to be the Christ will offend those who realize that he is satanic in his ambitions.

"Those who are rebuilding and learning to live harmoniously together will, for a time, stay out of his way, but as he becomes more dictatorial they will huddle in select groups to seek ways of curbing his power; and by the time he has slaughtered some of those who have offended him, they will have established a secret network of their own to put an end to his machinations."

Although the subject was gruesome, I asked the Guides if they could be more explicit, and they wrote: "The Antichrist will be thwarting the good efforts at every turn, demanding obedience to his orders in the name of God. Just as Jim Jones recruited followers in the name of God, but then began to pose as the Messiah himself, so will the Antichrist, on a greater scale, set himself up as the final arbiter. Those who would follow the dictates of their own conscience—that voice within—

will be sorely tried; and as his power expands they will form covert groups, for there will be too few policemen to watch all the doings, even in that decimated population. They will overcome him, as we said, and because of the private network that those good people have established to thwart the Antichrist, it will be easy then for all to be in touch with one another, and for the New Age to flower."

Recalling that the Guides had predicted the return of the gentle Lemurians, whose continent was destroyed in a similar shift of the axis eons ago, I asked for further comment on them, and the Guides declared: "Lemurians are among the Walk-ins already in physical bodies, and more and more of them will come in during the war of the late 1980s and beyond, ready to help people over the rough days ahead. Not all Walk-ins, of course, are Lemurians, but they are the finer elements of the ages past, and are of inestimable value in their understanding of the Flow, the energies, and the power of love."

Dismayed by the bleak prospects for the remainder of this century as depicted by the Guides, I asked what point there is in trying to solve the present ills of the world, or to create beauty, if so much of earth's treasure is to be destroyed within twenty years. Would not their predictions discourage people from even trying?

"The best way to view this," they replied, "is to consider a perfect prism. Sometime it will shatter, but is that less reason for enjoying its beauty so long as it is a delight to the senses? With the earth, it is even more important to create beauty and strive for harmony, because we are individual souls who together create a whole, and if we are ever to be reunited with the Godhead, it behooves us to strive each moment of the day for that harmony and well-being which can equip us for the reunion. To put it plainly, each moment spent in physical being is an opportunity for advancement of the soul's progress toward that goal, and until we master the art of love and forebearance, we are damaging the prospect for a perfect whole."

CHAPTER XVII

The Shift

A recent newspaper article distributed by United Press International began: "There will be six and a half billion people crowding Earth at the beginning of the 21st century, and the population is growing three to four times faster in Third World nations." Quoting a new study by the Environmental Fund, it said that by the year 2000 four people out of every five will be living in the underdeveloped countries of Asia, Africa, and Latin America, where the population "has grown by 92 percent since 1950."

These figures by demographers are causing alarm among social scientists and world politicians who wonder how these vast hordes can possibly be supported by backward countries that cannot even take care of the needs of their present populations.

If the Guides are correct in their assertions, that is at least one problem that will not have to be faced by the next generation. The World War of the late 1980s will substantially reduce the population, they say, and the survivors of the axial shift at the close of this century will number in the millions, rather than the billions.

"The shift will have its warnings," the Guides wrote one morning. "The weather will become increasingly violent, with heavy snowfalls, strong gales, and increased humidity. There will be rumblings beneath the earth, and the trees will sway. Shortly before the actual shift, there will be two specific types of warnings. The eruptions of ancient volcanoes in Mediterranean islands, South America, and California will result in pestilence, and shortly thereafter earth tremors of major proportions, affecting wide land-masses in northern Europe, Asia, and South America, will provoke tidal waves of monumental scope. These, then, will be the forerunners of the shift itself, and for days and nights beforehand the earth will seem to rock gently, as if soothing an infant in its trundle bed."

They said some will recognize this as the time to remove themselves quickly from the seacoasts and other exposed places, and while that exodus is occurring there will be increasing earthquakes, and volcanic eruptions in flat areas that had previously shown no sign of cones.

But not all will heed these "ominous signposts," as the Guides term them. "Some will remain de-

spite the alarms, disbelieving that a shift will occur; and some, deciding that it is a good time to
return to spirit, will refuse to leave their homes.
Remember that many will be so exhausted by the
war years that the spirit plane will seem attractive, particularly to those who long to join loved
ones who met physical death during the war. The
approaching shift of the axis will therefore seem
almost a relief to them. The scars of war and the
fratricide and hatreds of that warfare will so dev-
astate the people that there will be much to rec-
ommend the cleansing of the earth. Earthquakes
will herald the approach of the alteration, and
rumblings within the earth will presage the tu-
multuous day."

According to the Guides, the event itself will
occur "in the twinkling of an eye," as the earth
"slurps approximately onto its side.

"In daylight areas, the sun will seem to stand
still overhead, and then to race backward for the
brief period while the earth settles into its new
position relative to the sun," they declared. "Those
who are capable of reaching safety will see the
earth's surface tremble, shudder, and in some
places become a sea of boiling water, as the oceans
pour upon the land. Simultaneous explosions beneath the earth's crust will bring new land above
the surface of the waters, as other areas are swal-
lowed by the sea."

In graphic style, the Guides wrote: "We ask that
you picture a giant wave, higher than a ten-story
building, racing toward shore. Impossible to escape it, so in that moment of terror it is well to

put aside fear and think only of the good that is to come by passing into spirit. Conquer fear, and one has risen above the battle. Ferocious winds will howl across the land, and in areas that the sea does not reach it will be as if a comet had collided with the earth, toppling it out of its accustomed orbit. In nighttime areas, the stars will seem to swing giddily in the heavens, and as dawn breaks the sun will seemingly rise from the wrong place on the horizon."

Within the few moments during which some areas of our global earth are rotated away from the sun's rays, countless numbers of humans, animals, and birds will freeze to death. This is not an unprecedented event, since explorers today are finding the frozen remains of tropical vegetation and grass-eating mammals in a perfect state of preservation near the North Pole, which was once in a sunnier clime. Nor are the Guides predicting an event that scientists label impossible. Dr. Frank Hibben, an archaeologist with the University of New Mexico, says that 171 magnetic reverses of the earth have occurred during the last seventy-six million years; and explorer Maurice Ewing states that "the poles have switched position with some regularity for nearly a billion years—the present extent of the evidence." Both Edgar Cayce and the Guides have attributed the sinking of Lemuria in the Pacific Ocean to a shift of the axis, and agree that it will occur again at the close of this century, with dramatic reversals of climate as the globe partially revolves.

I asked the Guides to elaborate on the immediate effect of climatic changes on the survivors, and they wrote: "To those survivors who had been living in torrid areas, it will feel like refrigerated air sweeping all before it. But if the area was cold beforehand, the winds will feel like blasts from a fiery furnace. This effect will be temporary, and as the winds abate there simply will have occurred drastic climatic alterations. Those who previously were hot will now shiver, and vice versa. Since buildings in many areas will have been totally swept away, and even the trees felled as if by giant axmen, there will be little protective covering. All power lines will have snapped like jackstraws, severing communications and electricity, and those who must dispose of their fallen comrades will have their immediate work cut out for them. Those in caves and low-lying valleys between hills will have the best chance of escaping unscathed, so that entire families will survive. There will be some anguish and heartache, but also exhilaration in having withstood the ferocity of nature, and most of those remaining will feel that God saved them for a purpose."

The Guides say that many of those living east of the Appalachian Mountains will, as the time for the shift nears, "want to remove themselves to the other side of that natural barrier from the sea," but they added: "This is not to say that the entire east coast will be buried under a sea of water, but rather that some parts of it will become ocean bottom as the waters roll in, and New York City will vanish. Remember that Atlantis will be rising, so that this will tip parts of the east coast downward as the upheaval occurs beneath the seas.

"Florida will scarcely survive, except as scattered islands. The southern states bordering the Atlantic and Gulf of Mexico will be drastically altered, including parts of Texas. In the West, the remainder of California will disappear beneath the broiling waves, and the Great Lakes at some point will empty directly into salt waters. We do not wish to pinpoint every alteration in the earth's surface, but those who want to remain in physical body will be thinking of moving to inland areas before the shift. We do not mean that the elderly should flee the sunbelt. Rather, they should give serious thought to whether it is worth the effort to make drastic alterations in life-style in their declining years. When the shift occurs, Canada will be in a warmer latitude, and much of it will be relatively safe from sinking or destruction by tidal waves. Not a bad place to be, for those wishing to stay on in physical form."

Naturally I asked about Washington, D.C., and the Guides reported: "It will be devastated, but not totally destroyed, and since it is near the mountains, government workers will carry on in the previously prepared shelters there, beneath and within the solid rock. Virginia Beach will strangely survive, as most other seaside resorts disappear. Whole areas of the eastern and western United States, England, southern Asia, and Europe will be deluged by water as Atlantis emerges, and parts of Lemuria will rise in the Pacific Ocean, even as Hawaii slides into the sea. These areas will then be in a colder climate, while frozen wastelands in the northern reaches of Russia, Europe, and Canada will become warm and humid, providing immense acreage for the growth of food and animal life. Some landmasses will be under water for millennia, but the Russian and Chinese survivors will revolt against their oppressive governments and become new frontiersmen in the best sense of the word. They will be the hardy pioneers, and perhaps because of the oppression under which they have lived, they will set an example in self-reliance for those who had been accustomed to softer living."

Feeling acute distaste for the entire subject, I asked the Guides if they could think of anything pleasant to say. Almost as if they were chuckling to themselves, they replied: "Those who fear the event should think of the exciting movies they have watched, such as *Star Wars,* and realize that they will be privileged to witness one of the greatest events of all ages. It is like a marvelous solar flare that would bring all out of their houses to watch, and to tell their grandchildren about, so why not feel the same way when one is actually a part of the great happening?

"Those who survive will 'dine out on the story,' as the phrase goes, for the remainder of their lives, telling the new arrivals about it, and pointing out where there used to be land and now is water. Think of the thrill for those who have secreted themselves in caverns a hundred miles inland, to peer out the next morning and discover that they are now living beside the sea! Think of the survivors who will behold vast stretches of virginal land, where before the oceans rolled.

"Those who pass into spirit will also have had an electrifying experience, and how they reacted to it will hasten or deter their spiritual development. Those who tried to save themselves at the expense of others will have to live with that karmic blot for a long time, since opportunities to undo the harm by reincarnating will be scarce for thousands of years. But those who gladly gave their lives in trying to rescue others will 'score Brownie points in heaven," as the young people say. The Walk-ins will go and come, some surviving and others returning here, but those who remain in the flesh will be able to garner support to feed the populace, and clothe and house them, while setting them on a firmer path. There will be much to commend this experience, so do not think of it as a diabolical era. The earth is in a state of evolution. The shift will be a continuation of the growth of Planet Earth, even as we souls are in and out of physical form, each time with new shells to serve that particular incarnation. Remember that without growth and alteration there is death, and nothing dies."

The Guides concede that these last two decades will test the mettle of the fainthearted. "In order to achieve oneness with the Creator," they stressed, "one needs to polish his character, hone his talents, and shed the encumbrances that tend to hold him back from the greater freedom of the spirit realm. None who seeks that reunion needs fear the axial shift. Some will survive in flesh and others in spirit, and until one understands the purpose of the cleansing that results from a shifting of the earth's poles, he will be held back by fear."

Well, at least there is one who need not fear it, since the Guides say I will not be around when the shift occurs.

CHAPTER XVIII

Chaos and Cleanup

It's all very well for discarnate Guides who are untroubled by bodily ills to extol the virtues of cleansing the earth, but what of those millions remaining in human flesh who will have to face the devastation resulting from the shift?

If the Guides' predictions come to pass, everything that we term civilization will be utterly disrupted. Power stations, telephone lines, hydroelectric plants, office buildings, housing, dock facilities, and refineries will all have been swept away or rendered virtually useless. Food and fuel distribution will be impossible for some time, and although ample seeds may have been carefully stored in safe areas, several months are required to produce crops even in the temperate zone, and America will be much more frigid.

Anguishing for the survivors, I spoke to Michael about the predicted tragedy, and in comforting tones he replied: "The shift and the chaos are a very necessary process in order to prepare mankind for the next set of signposts in human evolution. That statement comes from Group Mind. Let me use a parable to illustrate this truth. Out here in the West, when a farmer prepares to plant a crop of spring wheat in September, he must do violence to the earth. He first takes a plow and breaks the ground in long furrows. Next he uses an instrument called a harrow, and with that set of spikes he violates the earth still further, and smooths it into soft lumps. Then he takes a seeder, which is a series of pipes and a long trough, and with it he drives slow-growing seed grain five or six inches into the earth, well below the frost line so that the tender new plants will not germinate too early and be killed by wintry cold. Planet Earth is like a field where weeds have grown up with the crop. A lot of the crop has to be plowed back under along with the weeds, to be converted into nutrient material, before a new crop can be planted. The coming shift is the plowing of the field called earth, and the farmer's name is Evolving Life. When the farmer tills and plows and harrows the ground, he is setting up proper conditions for a new crop. The shift will likewise set up conditions for a new crop of human life forms, so that returning entities can come in and carry forward the process of individual and racial evolution."

After digesting Michael's apt analogy, I sat down with Laura to try to picture how the world

would be for weeks and months after the cata-
clysmic shifting of the poles. We could visualize
the churning seas, the earth rumbles, the earthquakes and violent winds, the skyscrapers sway-
ing and crashing to the ground, the airplanes
splintering, the houses being picked up as if by
giant hands and flung in every direction, the dams
breaking and inundating everything in the path
of the torrential waters, the livestock and people
drowning together while fallen trees crush all before them. But after the fury of the storm abates,
what then?

"Cities will most likely be in utter chaos," Laura
began. "Assuming that some buildings are left
partially standing, survivors will be huddling in
whatever ruins remain, and scavenging for supplies of food left by the many who died. Those who
have hoarded food may be killed by hungry neighbors, as they try to defend their caches. If it is
warm, food will spoil quickly without refrigera-
tion, and rotting bodies will bring on pestilence.
If it is cold these problems will be less pressing,
but shelter and heat will be of immediate con-
cern."

And what about those who are not caught in
cities?

"Suburbs will be the first areas thronged by
weary refugees from metropolitan centers, where
rubble and disease have made living conditions
intolerable," Laura mused, "and families who try
to barricade themselves in what remains of their
houses can expect continual streams of hungry,
desperate human beings. Rural areas, where farm

families have learned to be more self-reliant than city people, will nevertheless be besieged by those tramping on foot through the countryside, scavenging for physical survival, and stealing to keep their bodies alive."

On a more cheerful note, Laura said thoughtfully: "But those who have worked together and learned early on to cooperate will find themselves in far better shape, whether they are in cities, suburbs, or country. After the destruction they will be seeking out one another to ensure their common survival, because it has become second nature for them to think in terms of the group. Beginning with the rescue of one another, they will band together and share what they have left. Each may sift through the ruins of his home to find tools, pans, food, clothing, and other basics to share, and they will pool their skills to start rebuilding shelter and planting vegetable gardens."

Those people who have previously worked together in community groups or communes will be better prepared to deal with vigilantes, roaming bands of refugees, thieves, and freeloaders. Such marauders could otherwise constitute such a dire threat that merely living in a safe area during and after the shift would be no insurance for survival.

Laura believes that many groups will respond with the inner knowledge they have acquired through cooperative living. "They will understand that when a conflict appears imminent, their own attitude and the power of love can neutralize anger and threat," she said. "They will also have learned to tell the difference between one who is truly in need and one who habitually sponges on others. They may decide that the best way to handle such refugees is to give them a meal and a night's lodging, and then send them on their way with encouragement and a small supply of food."

Some of the strays may bring with them skills that are needed, and be invited to join the groups. Some will bring news, and after being fed will offer to carry messages to other areas cut off from regular communications. The relationship between the settled groups and the roamers can thus alter from that of adversary to one of love and helpfulness. But where groups have become embroiled in inner conflicts and power struggles there will inevitably be trouble, because without harmony they cannot survive in a crisis situation.

My Walk-in friends say that those who have learned to rely on inner guidance and remain in the Flow will be "led" to havens of safety and to groups where harmony prevails. Those who have tested the Law of Manifestation should be able to visualize food, and find it in unexpected places. The gale winds accompanying the shift will scatter materials so randomly that those who heed the inner voice can find what they need, or a reasonable substitute.

The Walk-ins predict that this shakedown period will last for perhaps five years, during which time people will have grown accustomed to the altered seasonal patterns, and know when to seed for crops. They will have begun to rebuild more permanent housing and to establish a bartering system of trade. News will begin to arrive of growing stability in reconstructed cities, of the availability of new supplies, and of a gradually improving system of communication and commerce.

Since this material came from Walk-ins who are incarnate, I sought the Guides' view of the reconstruction period following the shift, and they wrote: "As to the aftermath, there will be some frenzied weeks while the survivors search for their friends and ferret out debris for reconstruction. Those who have buried a supply of nails, hammers, and simple tools like axes in safe areas will have a head start in reconstructing makeshift dwellings. And since some food and seeds will also have been safely secreted, famine will be avoided, because there will be fewer to feed. Acreage that had been planted before the shift will produce yields of underground foods such as potatoes, carrots, onions, and radishes, and many cellars stocked with edibles will survive the shift's fury. Goodwill in working together will produce an almost festive atmosphere, and while some will grieve for lost ones, others will set to work to rebuild and help others.

"As Laura has correctly foreseen, there will be some anguish in personal relationships, with the freeloaders and the greedy preying upon those who had foresight. Fortunately these deadbeats and spongers will gradually die out, for as we have said, a secret network will be developed among those who want to dispose of the Antichrist, and through this network the good people will learn to refuse aid to spongers. They will also be warned of the approach of thieving mobs, who will be killed before they can loot the stores of the workers, and the world will be well rid of them. They will have a long time in spirit to rue their evil ways."

I asked how surviving nations of the world will be able to establish contact with each other, and the Guides wrote: "New York City will, of course, have vanished beneath the sea, but after a time there will be new communications centers, and some of the previously elected officials will do what is necessary to establish a semblance of governmental order. As we have said, it will not be long thereafter until the Antichrist asserts himself, and keep in mind that he will already have an official position in the national government, so that he will not seem to be usurping power. Since he will have the ambition and imagination to seize control, he will move ahead more rapidly than others, until he is foremost among peers. Soon he will become nonpareil throughout the world, as he issues orders through radios operated by battery and solar energy."

This latter comment raised many questions in my mind. How can the Antichrist wield world power if he has no means of physical access to other parts of the globe? If there is no oil, how can airplanes fly between nations, in the event that some planes survive the havoc? If seacoasts are largely swept away, how can ships and supertankers dock, supposing that some of them survive?

I posed these questions to the Guides, and after

my meditation they replied: "Some ships will survive, and some oil as well. There will even be a
few survivors from the great armadas of jet planes,
and these will be reserved for governmental use
in communications and urgent rebuilding tasks.
Many shipping ports will be swept away, such as
those in New York, England, Le Havre, California, and others throughout the world, but some
will survive, and the shift will create beautiful
new natural harbors where ships can pull in to
unload some essentials. These will require a few
years to be totally usable, but during that time
the Antichrist will be establishing his position in
America, communicating by radio with other
parts of the world, and stepping up his drive for
recognition as the savior of the world.

"The Antichrist has returned in this era to
conquer the world religions, and set himself up as
the one and only savior of mankind. His is a fer-
vent mission, for this man will have learned nothing during the two thousand years since Jesus was
nailed to the cross. He will still view himself as
more mighty than emperors, and will be convinced
that he can rule the world forever. His power will
grow in such enormity that it will threaten all
mankind."

Fortunately, the Guides have already given assurance that his Machiavellian plottings will be
aborted. I asked how he will eventually meet his
doom, and my unseen friends replied: "He will be
captured, and hung without trial. This will not
seem shocking then, as it might now, for there
will be no courts that are free from his manipu-

lation. The will of the people is not manifest except through free elections, and these will not return to existence until after the death of the Antichrist."

Then, they said, the millennium will truly dawn.

The World to Come

The travails and heartaches predicted for the next few decades will not have been endured in vain, if the Guides correctly foresee the golden age to follow. That period, they say, will see the commencement of the millennium, as foretold in the Book of Revelations, when Christ returns to earth to usher in a thousand years of peace.

My unseen friends report that after the death of the Antichrist, free elections will be called throughout the world. "And as if by instinct all will wish to have the same kind of representative government, so that each area will choose delegates to a world body that will oversee the earth. Thus it will be one government and one world, and the new currency to be introduced will be usable anywhere. By that time a new kind of communication will have been established, with travel by spaceships throughout the globe, and magnetic and solar energies replacing fossil fuels."

The Guides say that the reincarnated Lemurians, who originated the science of agriculture when the earth was new, "will return to do that which they once performed so well, achieving harmony with natural forces and starting husbandry in new areas that once were beneath the sea."

"The twenty-first century will be a time of beatitude," they declared. "All beings will work together to rebuild the shattered earth and renew its fertility, which will have been drastically affected by the alteration of the earth's poles. New lands emerging from the seas will at first be saline, but will soon begin producing quantities of exotic foods, and a new type of agriculture will emerge. Some areas that once were fertile will have become arid deserts or sea bottoms, and others which had been overproducing due to artificial fertilizers will wisely be left fallow for a time. Thanks to the returning Lemurians, the ability to read minds through mental telepathy will spread rapidly, outmoding some communications systems, and a peaceful age will flower."

I asked how they will prevent warfare, and the Guides said that "through a form of transference of the soul-mind" leaders will be able to project themselves into strategy meetings in any area of the globe, and by learning of plans and intentions can "affirmatively voice aims that will dissolve the tensions.

"In the twenty-first century arms will become

virtually unknown," they declared, "for man will no longer seek strife and turmoil, and his neighbor will be as himself. This is indeed the millennium, as foretold long ago. It will return men's souls to rule by God's laws, and will see a resurgence of the love force that is the glue of the universe. When conflicting ideologies exist side by side there is strife, but when all are in agreement on how to govern and how to worship, there is quietude and peace. This, then, will be a momentous era well worth the anticipation of those who survive the shifting of the axis, and those who return to a new earthly turn of the wheel. It will be a time of tremendous spiritual advancement, as man turns his quest inward, rather than outward to technological advances that seem to ease the burdens of life, but in reality add immeasurably to those burdens."

One morning I had been musing on the wonders promised for the New Age, when the Guides typed: "If in a single day everyone would now lay aside all animosities, and put aside selfish motives, the world would be revolutionized by nightfall. Such is the power of souls acting together to effect favorable change! If man elected to do so, he could bring the twenty-first century's wonders to this pathetic century overnight, by deliberately altering his thinking. This will not occur in the present century, alas, but it will begin to occur in the next century, because after the shift of the axis, most will be cleansed of evil-thinking in the common desire to survive and rebuild. It is that manifestation [the shift] which will so shock humanity that man will devote himself to helping others as himself, and good thoughts will project to such an extent that it will seem like a new race of human beings. Actually, it is merely a demonstration of what right-thinking can do."

Miriam and Laura agree that the period of chaos and cleanup will eliminate many who were sickly and had relied on pill-popping instead of their inner reserves, as well as most of the freeloaders, the thieves, and the greedy. They say that the majority of those remaining in physical bodies will be healthy, strong, loving, kind, and sharing, because those are the resources that can withstand calamity and rebuild.

"Perhaps the vast destruction and turmoil will have been necessary in order for the next step in man's development to begin," Laura said musingly. "Sometimes a lesson about oneself is best learned when one loses everything material, and must rely on his inner self to survive in the physical world. I do know that as this new age of harmony dawns, it will be time for the current wave of Walk-ins to bow out."

Startled by this new thought, I telephoned Michael and asked for his comment. Corroborating what Laura had said, he declared: "The present wave of Walk-ins is here to lay the foundation for what is coming, so that a great number may survive. By laying the foundation, I mean helping other human beings to get a glimmer of awareness and to trust their intuition. As the New Age dawns, the number of new Walk-ins will diminish, because not nearly so many will be needed. Many of the Walk-ins now entering know that they aren't going to survive the shift. What's important is what they are to do *now*, and they're not worried by the fact that the bodies they borrowed are not going to survive. The important thing is to get that foundation laid during the next two decades. That is the reason they came back."

The Guides for many years have been prophesying that Christ will return to earth in human form during the twenty-first century. I asked if they could be more definite as to the timing, and they wrote: "The one who will prepare the body for the Christ Spirit will be born within two years after the Antichrist is put to death. We are not yet able to say where that birth will occur, for the world will look vastly different then as to geography, and latitude and longitude. He will be pure in heart and brave in spirit, and is returning for the sole purpose of living an exemplary life in a perfect body, so that when the Christ enters, there will be no sin to overcome."

I eagerly asked if he would be recognized as the Savior this time, and how long he would remain in physical body. "When the Christ enters it will be known to all," they said, "for so many signs will point to his coming that there will be no question this time. It will not so much require faith as knowledge, for in that benign era Walk-ins will be familiar sights, highly respected and admired. Thus the Christ Spirit will enter this perfect body and mind, and will rule over the hearts of man. There is no way to say at this time how long he will remain in flesh. That decision is his, and it would be like trying to out-guess God for us to speculate on it."

Because of their reference to Christ as a Walk-in, I pleaded for a fuller explanation of the Second Coming, and the Guides responded: "The Christ will come as a Walk-in just as he did before, entering the body of a perfected being who will come to prepare the way through birth. It is thus that 'immaculate conception' is understood on this side. We were not able to tell you that before, because you did not then know about Walk-ins, and might have doubted our veracity."

I asked if Jesus of Nazareth would again reincarnate, in order to "prepare the body for the Christ Spirit," and the Guides said that he would not. "It is difficult to explain the difference between Jesus and the Christ, since they are so intertwined in the Biblical accounts," they continued. "Jesus, the human being, was born to Mary and Joseph, having been conceived during a deep spiritual sleep; yet his emergence as the Messiah occurred at the time of his baptism, when the Christ Spirit entered. That was 'God made manifest.' Therefore, it is not the typical case of a Walk-in. Jesus did not withdraw at the time of baptism, but was glorified. In the twenty-first century, the soul of another perfected being will return to human incarnation, and the Christ Spirit will rejoin it after perhaps two or three decades, to commence the thousand-year rule of peace upon the earth. There will occasionally be some strife thereafter, but so easily settled as to seem like perfection in comparison with today's turmoils."

At this time, a curious coincidence seemingly occurred. I had been fretting about whether I dared to quote the Guides as saying that a different being than Jesus would prepare the body for the Second Coming. Would it offend all of those wonderful readers who are deeply religious in their beliefs? Actually, the Bible does not say that Jesus himself will return to physical body, but I felt it to be a touchy subject.

Then, in the mail, from my Walk-in friend Michael, I received a rather astonishing communication. He knew nothing of what the Guides had written, nor of my own indecision, unless Group Mind conveyed that intelligence to him; yet this is what he wrote: "It is said that he who will be called the Christ will arrive at the beginning of the new era, after the shift and after the chaos. But it will not be the man who was once incarnate and known as Yeshua, or Jesus. It will be another Wise One. If you do not believe this message from Group Mind, you can put the question to the Guides. This Wise One will give the next set of signposts to humanity, just as Yeshua left us a set of signposts, and it took two thousand years for humanity to begin to see the wisdom of what he was really saying. Helen Keller summarized that very well when she said, 'Your success and happiness lie in you.' That was the message of the man called Jesus, or Yeshua. He tried to tell human beings that there are abilities and powers within them that they don't know they have. And the next Wise One is going to show how to use them to get the most out of life in terms of their own happiness, and the welfare of the race, and their own individual evolution—and then to put up the next set of signposts."

After absorbing this message, and marveling at the remarkable timing, I asked the Guides if they would rephrase the Second Coming in the simplest possible terms, and they obligingly wrote: "In the next century, the one who returns will be as Jesus was, in that there will be no stain on his being. He will have been both man and woman in previous earth lives, with the deepest understanding of both, and after he reaches maturity the Christ Spirit will come, and blend with him. The twenty-first century will so improve the basic spiritual nature of mankind that there will then be understanding of these divine principles. We cannot be more specific now."

Projecting ahead to the latter part of the millennium, the Guides said that all those in physical body will be working harmoniously for the common good. "When one falls ill, others will send healing energies, and do his tasks until he recovers or passes on. There will be so little malice as to be almost nonexistent. Thought waves will project from one to another, some in directed channels specifically to someone needing assistance, but available for all to use if they pause to heed the voice within. This will seem normal in those times a thousand years hence, when the age of enlightenment has joined the two worlds of spirit and physical being. Those who go on into spirit will be able to project directly to those in flesh, and vice versa, so that there is an open passageway, and as the earth repeoples from its slim beginnings after the shift, there will be rejoicing at the opportunities for rapid soul advancement, and the gradual elimination of the necessity for returning to physical being."

I asked whether people in that age will remain in physical body for a shorter or longer period than now, and they said: "For as long as is needed to complete the lessons they have returned to learn. There will be such an understanding of death that a nostalgia for the spirit world will be with them, and they will do their best to complete their earth terms satisfactorily, so that they need not return again to Schoolhouse Earth."

Color lines, they said, will be eradicated, "because since the human soul is without color, skin tone has no meaning here. Government will be of one type, with all sending delegations to occasional world parleys, and as the population increases there will be smaller units to handle local matters, but these will scarcely be needed, because of the harmony among the people. National barriers will be nonexistent, as each strives for the good of all."

Naturally I wanted to know what would happen after the promised thousand years of peace, but the Guides replied: "Beyond that thousand years we are unable to predict, for it has not opened out, and may depend on factors thus far unknown to such earthlings as ourselves. It is not feasible to go beyond that period, for God's will is not shown beyond the millennium of which we speak."

And on that note, the Guides drew the curtain on the world to come.